DATE DUE

MAY 0 5 2010	
NOV 0 9 2010	
NOV 2 9 2016	

BRODART, CO.   Cat. No. 23-221

Child Abuse, Gender and Society

Routledge Research in Gender and Society

Child Abuse, Gender and Society

Jackie Turton

Routledge
Taylor & Francis Group
New York   London

First published 2008
by Routledge
270 Madison Ave, New York NY 10016

Simultaneously published in the UK
by Routledge
2 Park Square, Milton Park, Abingdon, Oxon, OX14 4RN

Routledge is an imprint of the Taylor & Francis Group, an informa business

Transferred to Digital Printing 2008

Typeset in Sabon by IBT Global

Library of Congress Cataloging in Publication Data
Turton, Jackie.
Child abuse, gender, and society / Jackie Turton.
p. cm.— (Routledge research in gender and society)
Includes bibliographical references and index.
ISBN 978-0-415-36505-5 (hardback : alk. paper) 1. Women child molesters 2. Child sexual abuse. I. Title.

HV6570.T87 2008
362.76— dc22   2007023947

British Library Cataloguing in Publication Data
A catalogue record for this book is available from the British Library

ISBN10: 0-415-36505-8 (hbk)
ISBN10: 0-203-01609-2 (ebk)

ISBN13: 978-0-415-36505-5 (hbk)
ISBN13: 978-0-203-01609-1 (ebk)

Contents

Acknowledgments

My first debt of gratitude must go to all the respondents, without whose cooperation there would be no book. I would also like to express my immense gratitude to Jacqui Saradjian, Michelle Elliott, and Pauline Lane, who encouraged me through the fieldwork.

I have a number of people to thank for their contributions and thoughtful guidance.

Professor Ian Craib supervised my original PhD work until his untimely death at the end of 2002. He offered me both intellectual and emotional support, enabling me to maintain a sense of perspective despite the very difficult and painful stories of abuse. Dr Maggie Lee, as co-supervisor, stepped into the breach following Ian's death, and I could not have finished this book without her academic stimulation, her constant faith in me, and her kindness.

I would like to express a special vote of thanks to Dr Eamonn Carrabine for his comments on the manuscript and the intellectual guidance he offered throughout. Also, my thanks must go to Professor Nigel South and Professor Loraine Gelsthorpe, who have been generous with their time by reading and commenting on draft chapters.

I want to thank my father Ray, and my children Gregory, Emily, and Sam. They have been a constant source of encouragement and support.

Finally, I would like to thank Dr Mike Turton. He sustained me throughout the whole writing process with his practical and personal support.

1 Introduction

> The word 'paedophile' conjures up a picture of a suspicious looking man in a dirty mack lurking around the school gate. Few would expect it to be used to describe a woman . . . but how else would you depict a woman who fondles children, has intercourse or oral sex with them, or penetrates them with objects? It makes uncomfortable reading, which is precisely why the issues of female sexual abusers continue to be swept under the carpet and disbelieved. A society that now accepts the existence of male paedophiles finds the concept of female abuse too repugnant to accept—particularly when the abuser is the mother. (Valios 2000, 28)

The sexual abuse of children has traditionally been perceived as a male crime, and statistics would appear to confirm this to be the case. In the main, it is men who sexually abuse children, and in the main those children are female. However, a significant minority of children are abused by female perpetrators, and it is the behaviour of these women that is the focus of this book.

There has been very little research concerning women who sexually abuse children and, apart from a handful of books (Bunting 2005; Denov 2004; Mendel 1995; Elliott 1993), much of the work that has been published has been either psychologically focussed analyses or victim accounts. Not that this work should be undervalued in any way, since a full understanding of child abuse relies on a multi-disciplinary approach to both theory and practice. However, this book attempts to place female perpetrators into social context by considering a sociological view of the abusive behaviour and the response of the individual actors concerned. There is not one view on this matter, nor indeed one way of seeing and analysing such deviant behaviour, but it is useful to develop a pathway through some of the complexities of sexually abusive adult–child relationships to enable an understanding of the social processes involved.

UNDERSTANDING CHILD SEXUAL ABUSE

To recognise the significance of child sexual abuse, it needs to be placed in social context alongside all abusive behaviours towards children. The media attention awarded to sexual abuse would suggest it has obtained a high ranking in the profile of victimisation, and this is despite the fact that physical abuse and neglect are by far the most risky for the young child. Criminal statistics show that child homicides run at an average of seventy-seven per year in the United Kingdom, and most commonly the adult offenders are those who 'care' for the victims (Coleman et al. 2006). Creighton and Tisser (2003) in their analysis found that the criminal statistics for 2000/2001 identified parents as the principle suspects in seventy-eight percent of child homicide cases. Infants under the age of one are at most risk, and this group has consistently presented as the most vulnerable to fatal abusive attacks (Saraga 2001). By contrast, while all child abuse has the potential to cause long-term emotional and physical injury (Driver and Droisen 1989), it is the exception rather than the rule to find that sexual abuse offers any immediate or life-threatening risk to the child (La Fountaine 1990). Yet it can, on occasion, provoke an instant public response and considerable professional concern (Jenkins 1998), and it is useful to consider why this might be the case.

The Seductive Child

Child sexual abuse has been on the public agenda since the 1980s when the stories from adult survivors were given a discursive space (Plummer 1995). However, these early revelations did little to enhance the plight of some children since explanations of the stories were based around common assumptions and popular myths about the abuse. For instance, the legacy of Freud and the fantasy of sexual abuse lived on within the public, and some professional, belief systems despite empirical evidence to the contrary (Finkelhor 1984). The denial of child sexual abuse was encouraged by the belief that the sensual seductiveness of young children—especially girls, rather than grooming, initiated adult–child sexual relationships (Finkelhor 1984), a belief that even extended to some of those within the judiciary (Smart 1989). The suggestion here is not necessarily a denial of the act but a belief that children not only consented to the sexual behaviour but also encouraged and seduced the adult abusers.

Alongside the undercurrent of denial and scepticism lay the notion that where sexual abusive behaviour did exist, there was no need for concern as it caused little harm to the child, as indicated by reports from some incest trials.

> In the case of attempted incest on a daughter aged eight and indecent assault on another daughter aged six, the court observed: 'he did not do

any permanent, serious harm to these girls. They have for example each of them retained their virginity.' A probation order was substituted for a four-year sentence of imprisonment. (Mitra 1987, in Smart 1989)

Such a ruling continued to emphasise the patriarchal obsession with female purity by downgrading any abuse that left the female child intact. But where sexual intercourse occurred the child was in danger of being made culpable for her own victimhood.

Notions of the seductive child and the innocuous nature of sexual abuse have been robustly challenged by academic feminist inquiry (Walklate 1989; Smart 1989; Rush 1980; Miller 1987; Armstrong 1978, 1990) alongside such practical innovations as the Rape Crisis Federation[1] and ChildLine[2], which offer us a less expurgated view of the child's world. Not surprisingly, there has been some backlash within the revelations of so-called 'false memory' (Walklate 1989). However, there is now little dissent from the idea that child sexual abuse exists and that some adults—usually male—are predatory towards children. What remains more difficult to believe or accept is that a considerable number of these predatory adults are family members and, even more difficult, that a minority are female.

The Innocent Child

While on the one hand there exists the notion of the seductive, sexually and socially aware child, on the other we have created childhood as separate and different from the rest of society. We have reinforced this otherness with structures and systems that encourage and emphasise the distinctions rather than the similarities between children and adults. Children have been studied and analysed as different, allowing us to group them as 'special-isms' (Weeks 1989), rather than considering them, alongside adults, as part of the social whole. Children are observed, categorised, and counted but not asked, listened to, and included (Butler and Williamson 1994).They are researched, but their lived experiences are at best undervalued and at worst totally excluded.

We have developed fields of expertise in terms of psychological and physical development dictating time scales and achievements to highlight ideal types of progress and ideal types of children. It is not only a process that constructs the ideal child but also one that dictates how we should parent. While there have been some challenges to this linear developmental approach (Morss 1996), it remains the dominant view of children and childhood in the Western world.

We can link the development of professional expertise with the changes within families during the last century. In the United Kingdom we now have fewer children within families, some couples choose not to have children at all, and for other couples unable to conceive modern technology may be exploited to the full, through infertility treatments, in vitro fertilization

(IVF), and surrogate motherhood. So, whether through controlling or stimulating fertility, the child has become overly precious, in need of constant observation, care, and protection. While recognising the real dangers that do beset children we ought to be aware that keeping them dependent and fearful does not help the goal of child protection (Scott, et al. 1998). Weeks (1989) explains how the desire to protect children is interlinked with the way in which we have created them as specialisms.

> A conceptualisation of the separateness of children went hand in hand with the socially felt need to protect their purity and innocence. They became a form of property to be admired and cuddled, to be cared for and above all protected.(Weeks 1989, 48)

It is not just an emotional bond that has caused a protective response. The ever-increasing number of situations identified and labelled as risky means that parents have to be more cautious, protective, and controlling of their children, as much to avoid public disapproval and the social police as to ensure the safety of the child (Pain 2006). Furthermore, the separation between adult and child not only offers a sense of identity through difference, but also ensures a long-term, intimate relationship, which may be important when considering familial abuse.

> Collectively and individually, we look to 'the Child' to give meaning and coherence to our lives, to tell us who we are and what we hold dear, to provide a bulwark against the encroaching tides of change, and to reassure us that at least some of our social connections are fixed, indissoluble and beyond contract. But children only provide us such assurance so long as we can be certain of their fundamental difference from ourselves. Thus we insist upon the innocence, dependency, helplessness and asexuality of 'the child' and dread the 'paedophiles' . . . who would defile it. (O'Connell Davidson 2005, 10)

The result is that children are invariably excluded from even the decision making that directly affects their lives. Adults, often parents, decide 'what is best' based on expert opinion and their own past experiences and memory, without considering the child's point of view. Thus we have an ambiguous situation in which many children are legitimately kept ignorant and powerless, leaving them vulnerable and poorly equipped to protect themselves. As Jenkins suggests,

> to protect is also to assert control, and to declare that young people are children is to state that they are and should be limited in their proper scope of individual action . . . by definition it is to deny such a person the full rights of choice appropriate for an adult.
>
> (Jenkins 1998, 225)

Childhood innocence and vulnerability feeds into the grooming process[3] becoming part of the victim's identity (Warner 2001), creating further opportunity for abuse by acting as a 'source of titillation for abusers' (Kitzinger 1997, 168). Given this observation, the question arises whether the maintenance of an 'innocent' child is in fact 'largely created, maintained and defined by adults for their own reasons' (Gittens 1998, 151).

Paradoxically, the sexually aware child, the child who has lost innocence, may also lose her right to protection because her seductive nature and understanding renders any sexual acts perpetrated on her body less abusive and somewhat 'less of a crime' (Walklate 1989; Kitzinger 1997).

The discourses of parental protection and childhood innocence maintain the home and the family as the haven from a harmful outside world and dangerous strangers. It is in this environment that public images of the sexual predator emerge.

The Fear of Stranger Danger

'The real horror is the fact that child abuse, like murder, is largely a domestic crime' (Young 1993, 108). Despite this fact, in the current climate of the risk society (Beck 1992), public blame is fixated on the psychopathic stranger (Jenkins 1998). It is this 'stranger danger' description that has political benefits, which do not just reinforce the family structure (Jenkins 1998) but reinforce a heterosexual, male-dominated environment. The misconception is that this ideal type of family social structure protects children through the incest taboo (Bell 1993), thus creating a world of perpetrators who are other and reconfirming the power and control of parents. It is of course, very comforting to rationalise child sexual abuse as an event that occurs outside of the family setting; it becomes more acceptable, understandable, and believable and therefore easier to manage.

> Dangerous outsiders have attracted a vastly disproportionate share of official attention, precisely because they represent the easiest targets for anyone wishing, however sincerely, to protect children. (Jenkins 1998, 238)

In the late modern world, when much of the emotional labour of families (Gittens 1998) is based around the protection of children from psychological and physical harm, the horror of child abuse offers ideal opportunities for media hype and moral panic[4] (Thomas 2000; Cohen 2002). Much of our common knowledge is developed from a combination of research theory, everyday conversation, and media reports, and these determine how we make sense of child abuse (Warner 2000). Furthermore, it can be the media interest itself that accentuates public concern when the abuse is sexual because it removes the moral innocence that is considered so precious for children, even though it may be this very innocence, this lack of knowledge, that renders the child vulnerable to exploitation (Gittens 1998). Perhaps more importantly, media tales tend to overreport and overemphasise stranger abuse, encouraging the mythical public perception of safe families and dangerous streets (Saraga 2001)[5]. Furthermore, the current demographic displacement of a rising elderly population also results in raised anxieties about child protection and the nature of risk concerning child abuse (Jenkins 1998).

So, recognising that most sexual abuse occurs within the home remains a difficulty for the public and media alike. Although the academic literature has moved sexual abuse from the danger of strangers to the intimacy of incest, relocating child sexual abuse from 'public drama to private drama' (McIntosh 1988), it is still much easier to perceive perpetrators as something other and not like us! The continuing vilification of the few known paedophiles, encouraged by the media, confirms that this myth continues within our late modern technological society and can lead to what Showalter labels *hystories*.

> The cultural narratives of hysteria, which I call *hystories*, multiply rapidly and uncontrollably in the era of mass media, telecommunications, and email. (Showalter 1997, 5)

One of the reasons child sexual abuse is such a high profile moral panic is that the risk to children of stranger attack is perceived as very high, despite the low probability rating (Cohen 2002). As we will see later, this factor is intrinsically linked to blame.

> The perception and acceptance of risk is intimately tied to the question of who is perceived to be responsible for causing the hazard or damage to whom. (Cohen 2002, xxvi)

As long as paedophiles who are strangers dominate the agenda, there will be a constant demand for more public surveillance and tighter laws; but acts of incest are more common and are more sociologically important. They are produced and reproduced within the normal social order of the family structure and could therefore help to provide 'a key to a sociological understanding of social structure and culture' (Bell 1993, 3).

Child Protection Discourse

The public and professional responses to child sexual abuse are constructed within particular discourses concerning the family, the innocent child, and the unknown abuser, and they are reinforced by a set of cultural norms that offer us specific ways of seeing the world (Reavey and Warner 2003). Social and cultural meanings are allocated to experiences and contexts that invariably position the social actors involved in familiar ways (Gavey 1999). Warner (2001) suggests that the reality of child sexual abuse itself is regulated not just by the act(s) but also by the intervention of agencies, societal reaction, and the way in which abusive experiences become naturalised, creating normative assumptions that function as social facts. Where child sexual abuse exists, the dominant discourse is of heterosexuality, incest taboo, and the assumption of male stranger perpetrators, leaving alternative possibilities outside of the box (Jenks, 1996). Thus, perceptions of the sexual offender and child sexual abuse become heavily weighted with meaning and expectation, taking for granted a universalism that renders difference such as gender, sexuality, ethnicity, or culture as invisible (O'Dell 2003) and falling back on the normalcy of the dominant sexually aggressive male within the heterosexual family order.

There are other difficulties hidden within the language used in child protection discourse.

> The simple phrase *child protection* is multilayered with complex rhetorical implications for family control and individual responsibility.
> (Jenkins 1998, 225; italics added)

Child sexual abuse has taken a generic meaning that covers a vast range of activities from the minor to the pathologically violent. This line of continuum may be a useful way of considering sexual offences, especially if applying an escalation theory. However, some academics would suggest that there is little evidence that sex crimes are linked in a logical chain (Jenkins 1998).

Even with academic projects there is very little consistency, and many literature reviews of child sexual abuse agree that there are wide variations within definitions (Bullock et al. 1995; Ghate and Spencer 1995), especially where female perpetrators are concerned (Hislop, 2001; Fromuth and Burkhart, 1987), making any useful comparative study or cumulative knowledge base at best complicated and at worst impossible.

So, in reality, sexual abuse is regulated through the child protection discourse that tends to 'naturalise' the experience and create normative assumptions about the identity and roles of men, women, children, and abusive practices.

> The ways in which laws are conceived, crime is reported and stories are constructed are not neutral, but rely on unacknowledged assumptions regarding issues such as sexuality, gender, race, ability and in respect of child abuse, childhood. These unacknowledged assumptions reinforce normative categories of identity regarding . . . the proper roles of men women and children and . . . structure the ways in which we can understand both sexual abuse and domestic violence.
> (Warner 2001, 5)

The Legacy of Gender Issues

'Until as late as 1990, it was taken as fact that all child sexual abusers were male' (Young 1993, 109). Add this assumption to the discursive restrictions and for many it is just too difficult to contemplate the female abuser. Apart from the social identification of women with the nurturing and mothering roles, the foundation of our current deconstruction of child sexual abuse has been based upon the presumption of the male perpetrator. It was in the 1980s that the modern 'discovery' of child sexual abuse and incest was publicly recognised. The political debate was initiated, almost simultaneously, by the child protection lobby and the women's movement and encouraged by the public acceptance of the sexual stories of victims (Plummer 1995). While both of these groups acted on the premise that child sexual abusers were male, their focus displayed some significant differences (Jenks 1996). For instance, the child protection lobby identified incest as family dysfunction and encouraged resolution by family therapy. The main emphasis in this approach is to preserve the existing family order, though there was no attempt to consider any concerns of imbalance of power within the family unit. As a consequence, this stance has been inclined to disperse the blame for abusive behaviour away from the perpetrator and distribute it within the family, often at the feet of the mother, although this perspective has lost favour in recent years.

The women's movement has, regardless of the considerable variety of feminist standpoints, attributed incest to the socialisation of men in terms of masculinity, power, and aggression. They challenged the notion of family dysfunction and mother blaming by the suggestion that abusive behaviour occurred because of the asymmetry of power in terms of age and gender.

Thus, both the feminists and the child protectionists excluded most female abusers. The child protectionists blamed the mother when incest occurred, not because she had committed an abusive act but because she failed to protect the victim. The feminists claimed sexual abuse as a gender issue concerned with ideas of socialisation, male roles, and masculinity. The importance of these two approaches, as we will see within this book, is that they form the backdrop upon which much of current child protection practice is based, and they legitimise social stereotypes of masculinity and femininity that can become a stumbling block to understanding female perpetrators. As a result of these converging views, there has been considerable opposition to any research or discourse concerning the sexual abuse of children by women[6]. Even amongst survivors there is an understanding that the dominant view of heterosexuality, femininity, and masculinity forms stumbling blocks to the acceptance of familial female perpetrators and especially sexual acts between mothers and daughters.

> I feel it is important for the general public to know that mother/daughter sexual abuse is not as easily identified as with a male perpetrator. The heterosexual view of sexuality limits the ability for people

to identify the abuse that a woman can perpetrate. (a survivor in Rosencrans 1997, 20)

Furthermore, encouraging the image of the male aggressor can fail to address difficulties for male victims, which are further complicated by the 'belief that sexual interactions between older females and juvenile males do not constitute abuse' (Mendel 1995, 30). While both male and female victims could benefit, a disengagement of heterosexualism and masculinity from sex crimes is a bit like 'imagining boats without water' (Rosencrans 1997, 19).

It is impossible to separate the social discourse developed around sexuality and childhood from the rationale of child sexual abuse. All of these factors enable us to disengage with the concept of the female perpetrator. I want now to highlight two myths that further colour our ideas about the existence of sexually abusive women.

MYTHS ABOUT FEMALE PERPETRATORS

The first myth is a question of denial: real women don't abuse, do they? It is perhaps easy to exclude and excuse women who can be categorised as masculinised or sick, but despite evidence to contrary, the abuse committed by women who fall outside of these groups is denied or minimised. As Welldon[7] has found, women who sexually abuse children, even those who seek help, may not be taken seriously.

> People simply do not want to know. . . . when as man admits to the group that he has committed incest, everyone is angry with him and shows hard feelings, a reflection of attitudes in society. When a woman says, always in a tentative manner, that she has funny feelings about her daughter, wants to touch her sexually very much and so on, everyone in the group says 'not to worry! It's just maternal instinct. It's perfectly natural.' (Welldon, cited in Search 1988, 83)

The importance of denial and the how, why, and where it occurs, forms the backbone of the analysis in this book and uncovers some important results.

In this introduction, however, I want to briefly consider what evidence we have for the actuality of female abusers. Using criminal statistics is clearly not sufficient, since many male abusers and most female do not reach the criminal justice system. Grubin (1998) identified that the official statistics show that women committed less than one percent of all sex offences, and in 2002/2003 women made up four percent of all arrests for sexual offences (Home Office 2003). These official figures are very low, and part of the reason is because until recently there has been a double gender standard.

whereby relationships between an adult woman and an underage boy have always been regarded as far less reprehensible than those in which gender roles are reversed. (Jenkins 1998, 14)

Any acts involving female adults and juvenile boys have been considered risky for authorities to pursue to prosecution, although the new Sexual Offences Act (2003)[8] may change this situation.

Although female abusers are grossly underrepresented in research litera-ture, a small number of studies conducted with abusers do offer some ideas of prevalence rates (Russell and Finkelhor 1984; Allen 1990; Elliott 1993; Sar-adjian 1996; Hislop 2001; Bunting 2005). Saradjian (1996) estimated that one percent of all children suffer serious sexual assault by an older female in childhood, and she suggested that this is probably an underestimate due to low disclosure rates. More conservative estimates have been proposed by Russell and Finkelhor (1984), who determined from their research that twenty percent of abused boys and five percent of abused girls suffer sexual abuse at the hands of a woman. Turner and Turner (1994), within their review of the literature, suggested that between six percent and fourteen percent of all substantiated cases of child sexual abuse in the United States of America involved female perpetrators. More recently, Bunting's (2005) analysis quotes 'current understanding suggests that females may account for up to five percent of all sexual offences against children' (p. 14).

These figures certainly indicate that this is a problem that we cannot ignore, but they raise questions for some who feel that the data regard-ing female perpetrators is biased by underrepresentation and under-report-ing (Justice and Justice 1979; Plummer 1981; Banning 1989; Rowan et al. 1990) and the numerous methodological anomalies.

Difficulties in methodologies between studies that attempt to estimate the percentages of female among sex offender populations make them difficult to compare . . . though it is difficult to estimate the percent-age of females in the child molester population, current studies indi-cate that, without question, the population of child molesters includes women. (Hislop 2001, 74)

It is not just inadequate methodologies and lack of appropriate ques-tions that can lead to any underreporting. Apart from the sexual abuse of children being the antithesis of expected female behaviour, offenders are likely to be embedded with family systems, rendering their actions unobserved or not recognised as sexual or abusive (Rowan et al. 1990; Saradjian 1996).

Other researchers argue that the vast majority of child abusers are male; women are far less likely to sexually abuse children. The reasons offered are based on the differential socialisation of males and females within Western society. So Finkelhor (1984) suggests that women are in general more mature, more self-controlled, and more empathetic than men, while La Fountaine (1990) observes that women are less influenced by society to find children sexually attractive, and many feminists define patriarchy, male power, and control as the overriding causal factors.

It may be that victim disclosures offer us a more accurate account. In 1992 a helpline, set up by a local radio station to complement the first national conference on female sexual abusers in London, received 100 calls from victims of female sexual abusers in the first 24 hours. Ninety percent of these victims had never talked to anyone before (Elliott 1993), indicating the hidden rate of this type of crime. Perhaps the most useful victim surveys come from ChildLine. During the year ending March 1991, ChildLine received 8,663 calls from victims of sexual abuse; 780 (about nine percent) of these cited a woman as their main or sole abuser (Elliott 1993); figures for 2001–2002 reveal that 'thirteen percent of the 8,402 children counselled in relation to sexual abuse reported the involvement of a female perpetrator' (Bunting 2005, 12). Obviously, we have to be wary of all statistics, even victim accounts.

> Reporting rates are . . . likely to be influenced by the context of the abuse, the victim's feelings about the experience and whether they think they are likely to be believed. (Ford 2006, 16)

However, suffice it to say here that for the purposes of this study these figures, both victim disclosure rates and research estimates, give a clear indication that the sexual abuse of children by female perpetrators does occur and is not limited to a few 'dysfunctional' women.

The second myth I want to dispel in this introduction concerns 'harm.' Even when the sexually abusive behaviour of women is believed, any possible harm to the child victim has traditionally been met with scepticism. After all,

> that she might seduce a child into sex play is unthinkable and even if she did so what harm could she do without a penis. (Mathis 1972, 54)

I think from the outset we have to understand that child sexual abuse has little to do with penetration, or at least little to do with penile penetration (Allen 1990; Rosencrans 1997). Sexual abuse involves anything from voyeurism, exhibitionism, pornography, and prostitution to masturbation, oral stimulation, penetration with objects, buggery, and rape. So we have a set of behaviours that in one way or another could involve either a male or a female abuser.

Although we should be wary of assuming a universal story of 'harm' (O'Dell 2003), all victims of sexual abuse can suffer some physical and emotional harm, and this is obvious when we consider the type of abusive behaviour that can occur. What many researchers have suggested in the past, however, is that child victims of male perpetrators suffer more significant harm (Allen 1990; Mendel 1995; Rosencrans 1997).

Some research findings (Russell 1984) suggest that the sexual abuse by women is less likely to be violent and sadistic and that the threats used to keep child victims silent are more subtle. On occasions this behaviour can be redefined by professionals as either unintended or 'not meaning any harm' (Denov 2004, 79).

Lawson (1993) suggests that female abuse falls into a number of categories forming a line of continuum. At one end she identifies subtle abuse that is noncoercive and nongenital and thereby considered less harmful. In cases of incest, it is possible that this behaviour is perhaps committed as the result of the mother's own unconscious need for sexual gratification or as an extension of the special attention given to satisfy the child's needs. Under these circumstances such behaviour may be disguised as child care (Groth 1979; Plummer 1981), since women have a licence to be intimate (O'Carroll 1980), and a high degree of physical contact between young children and women is expected as part of the female role (Plummer 1981).

The other end of Lawson's continuum recognises the sadistic sexual behaviour only occasionally displayed by female abusers.

> Some of the most tragic examples of this form of abuse have been described in the life histories of several serial sexual killers of females. One such killer was brutalised by his mother who sodomised him with a broomstick. (Lawson 1993, 266)

Ramsey-Klawsnik, 1990 (cited in Mendel 1995) also found that both male and female offenders perpetrated severe acts of sadistic sexual abuse. She recorded incidences such as burning, biting, pinching breasts and genitals, all committed by female perpetrators. All of these findings rather play down the suggestion that female sexual abuse could be confused with childcare, considered harmless or subtle. For instance, Sgroi and Sargent found in their research that

> all seven of (their) adult female clients reported a perception that sexual abuse by a first-degree female relative (mother or sister) was the most shameful and damaging form of childhood victimisation they had suffered. (Sgroi and Sargent 1993, 23)

And, as the stories from this research suggest, female perpetrators do commit grossly violent sexual acts.

> Jeff was abused by an older married woman who was his baby-sitter. She used objects to penetrate him and sat on his face, forcing him to perform oral sex.

Ann was sexually abused by her mother's friend, who also was her childminder. The nature of the sexual abuse included indecent photography, fondling, anal and vaginal penetration, administration of enemas and douches, and mutual masturbation.

"She started getting me up in the night to go to the lavatory and if I'd wet the bed, which I had most often than not, she would stand me in the bath. She didn't shower me down, she would put the actual hose inside my back passage, turn the tap on, tell me to lie on my back and she put it in the front, and told me to hold it. If I let go, I would get another belting." (Louise)

One of the most significant concerns regarding the long-term harm that may be inflicted by female sexual abusers was highlighted in some research projects concerning male sexual offenders. Groth (1979) found that sixty-six percent of the rapists in his study reported child victimisation by female perpetrators. Petrovich and Templar (1984) found that fifty-nine percent of rapists in their study had been sexually abused by a female. Briere and Smiljanich's (1993) data from a self-report survey found,

among the sexually abused men who reported sexual aggression against women, 80% had been sexually abused during childhood by a female perpetrator. In other words, sexual activity during childhood with an older female strongly predicted later sexual aggression against adult women . . . childhood sexual victimisation by females is a particular risk factor for later assault directed at adult female victims. (summarised in Mendel 1995, 62)

Cavanagh Johnson (1989) also noted in her literature review a number of studies that concur with Mendel's observation and suggested that it was important to note 'the high percentage of the most aggressive male sexual perpetrators who were molested by women' (p. 572).

It is important to recognise that sexual offences committed by women should not just be viewed as 'male-like' behaviour (Renzetti 1999); these offences need to be considered in context, taking into account power differentials and the restrictions of gendered structures, alongside an analysis of the rationale of the offenders. Nevertheless, the sexual abuse of children by women is hardly an insignificant matter, and it can be denied, excused, and minimised.

RESEARCHING SENSITIVE TOPICS

Regardless of the gender of the perpetrator, sexual abuse is a sensitive research topic. It is invariably a hidden crime, even more so where the abuser is female, and it is the covert nature of the deviant behaviour that silences both offenders and victims and challenges the expectations of the professionals involved. Whatever the topic, sensitive research tends to pose some particular threat—sometimes to the participants and sometimes to the researcher—and on occasions the threat of more widespread social and political implications (Lee and Renzetti 1993). Sexual behaviour in general, and intimate abusive or violent behaviour in particular, are private crimes, and as Lee and Renzetti suggest, any research activity can raise anxieties about the fear of identification, stigmatisation, or incrimination. By relating their life stories and their sexual experiences, abusers make themselves vulnerable to public exposure, attack, and ridicule and the abused to the memory of trauma, both emotional and physical. However, this does not mean that we should shy away from such undertakings.

> Sensitive research addresses some of society's most pressing social issues and policy questions. Although ignoring the ethical issues in sensitive research is not a responsible approach to science, shying away from controversial topics, simply because they are controversial, is also an avoidance of responsibility. (Sieber and Stanley 1988, cited in Lee and Renzetti 1993, 11)

It is not just ethical issues that create difficulties. We need to be aware of the context of storytelling. Events that occurred in childhood will now be interpreted within our adult experience, and much of our memory recall depends upon particular events and their impact on our lives. Often these stories may have been told and retold or at least mentally rehearsed[9]. The problem for child abusers and their victims is that everyday occurrences tend not to be as easily recalled as unusual or milestone events. Re-occurring life events tend to get bundled together in storytelling (Gottfredson and Hindelang 1977). So, for instance, survivors of child abuse may have been abused over a long period of time. Therefore, questions like 'When did it start?' and 'When did it stop?' may have no real meaning, and it is likely that one abusive event merges into another.

Another difficulty about relating events, peculiar to child sexual abuse, is False Memory Syndrome (FMS). FMS has brought adult disclosures of childhood sexual abuse into disrepute and has had a knock-on effect on the credibility of child victims. It occurs in the therapeutic situation when allegedly, repressed, previously unrecognised memories of childhood sexual experiences may emerge. There is little doubt that false allegations have occurred, but there is more hidden child sexual abuse than there are false claims (Saradjian 1996; Mendel 1995; Elliott 1993). Although the truth of any story is always open to interpretation, this book is focussed on the relationships between victim, abuser, and professional and their perceptions rather than the abusive act itself, and in any event none of the victim respondents involved had ever forgotten their childhood abuse. It is also important to note the findings of Williams (1995) that suggests repressed memories are more likely to be associated with dissociation then a false memory[10].

The other concern relating to studies of female sexual abusers, and violent women more generally, is the genuine fear that declaring 'women do it too' encourages antifeminist backlash and as such has the potential to undermine all the successful awareness-raising work achieved by feminists over the last three decades or so concerning domestic violence, rape, and child sexual abuse (Renzetti 1999). However, we can overcome this by openly recognising that some women do commit sexual and violent crimes and thereby grant these women—and I suggest by default all women—at least some agency and responsibility over their lives (Worrall 2002), as well as taking a feminist approach to the research and theorising.

> By taking ownership of the tasks of researching and theorizing women's use of violence, feminists can at once lay bare women's strengths and women's suffering, a process that I think will both empower women and harness the backlash. (Renzetti 1999, 52)

The data for this book were drawn from a series of in-depth interviews with offenders, victims, and child protection professionals including police officers, social workers, probation officers, counsellors, and health workers. The eight survivors were all adults and accessed through various gatekeepers including counsellors and clinical psychologists. Not surprisingly, the offenders were more difficult to access; apart from anything else, there are few of these women within the criminal justice or counselling systems. Ultimately, three women were interviewed over a number of sessions and while not a sufficient sample for any useful comparisons between offenders, their stories share a space with those of the survivors and the issues and case studies discussed by child protection workers. Many of the stories involved perpetrators who were either mothers or mother figures at the time of the sexual abuse.

CONCLUSION

This chapter has introduced the problem of female perpetrators of child sexual abuse. I have outlined the social construction of the child and how this influences the ways that risk and protection are perceived. I have considered the current focus on stranger-danger that has been encouraged by high-profile media attention and the way it feeds into our need to cast the blame for deviant behaviour on to others, while ignoring abusive behaviour that occurs within the family. Myths about women and the questionable nature of harm they can afflict on children casts doubts and sets the scene for the denial and minimisation of female perpetrators.

I will consider the denial and minimisation within this book as well as the rationale used to excuse women who abuse. Throughout the course of the work I have realised that women who abuse are excluded from the discourse and are often silenced[11], a silence that often encompasses their child victims as well. I have constantly been made aware by the stories told that our difficulty in understanding women who sexually abuse children is immersed in our own social, moral, and sexual selves. The following chapters endeavour to highlight how we have ignored the female abuser, her story, and her victims in the hope that we can find ways to break the silence.

> Child abuse is everyone's issue. However ardent and radical one's commitment to feminism, however painful the realisation that some women whose battles we fight are sexually abusing children, however small the incidences are, however caring and compassionate we may be, the fact that women are capable of sexual abuse is not going to go away, and we as women, whether feminist or not, can no longer deny it. (Young 1993, 111)

2 Putting Child Sexual Abuse into Context

As we have briefly considered in the previous chapter, child sexual abuse is a complicated subject that requires some demystifying and deconstructing if we are to begin to comprehend the problems that surround female perpetrators. Here we have not just one single set of behaviours but a range of social constructs that are influenced and reinforced by emotional outbursts and moral constraints. Attempting to consider all of these issues is beyond the scope of this book. However, I want to draw together some of the theoretical tensions that exist in order to find a social context for women who sexually abuse in order to locate the rationale and explanations of such behaviour.

This chapter considers the legal framework that dominates the child protection system and how cultural attitudes are focussed away from the female sexual abuser by the family structure and gendered social roles. I will critically assess the contributions and omissions of the feminists, taking into account their original resistance to consideration of sexually violent women and some of the more contemporary feminist ideas.

THE BUSINESS OF PROTECTING CHILDREN

One of the first difficulties encountered in connection with child sexual abuse is how to define acts that are so diverse. Sexual abuse, especially if the perpetrator is female, can emerge as very subtle behaviour (Etherington 1996) that has sexual overtones for the actors but may appear innocent or at the very least ambiguous to any outsiders.[1] Yet defining the act is an essential tool for research methodology and important if we are to consider issues of child protection, policies for practice, and legislation.

Perhaps a primary consideration is what do we understand by the term 'sexual abuse.' On the surface, this may seem a fairly simple process since we can all produce personal interpretations that appear to fit the description, but one of the problems for child protection is a general lack of consensus about definitions of sexual abuse. What do we include and what do we leave out? Do we just consider the physical 'sexual contact' as abusive and, if so, what about noncontact behaviour such as encouraging children to watch pornography and sexual acts or photographing children in various sensual poses or states of undress? These social conundrums create difficulties, especially for those working in child protection as well as those in the criminal justice system—a situation not aided by the re-sorting, reshuffling, and reattribution between the social and the experiential, the legal and the psychological definitions of child sexual abuse (Smart 1989). Furthermore, because different studies use different criteria (Bolen, et al. 2000; Cossins 2000), gathering any meaningful statistical data about child sexual abuse is bound to be met with complications.

In some ways, the development of an army of experts has caused further confusion over definitions. We have constructed a whole child-protection industry with hierarchies and bureaucracies that include experts from the various organisations connected with social services, health, education, the police, and others. Specialists require policies and procedures for action, and they rely on the objectivity of these for the business of protecting children. In the face of depleting resources and increasing demand, 'hierarchies of abuse' have developed, often based on gendered assumptions and rating acts of abuse in terms of predictions of harm to the victim. As a consequence, the victim's reaction and her or his subjective experience may become less significant within the grinding mechanisms of an industry of child protection.

Our pursuit of the protectionist approach reinforces the dilemmas and difficulties. Child protection enquiries from those suggesting overzealousness and lack of procedures, such as the Cleveland enquiry[2] (Department of Health and Social Security [DHSS] 1988), to those suggesting lack of expert supervision and training, such as the Victoria Climbie enquiry[3] (Laming 2003), and the demand for public information as to the whereabouts of known paedophiles, as in the aftermath of the Sarah Payne murder (*Guardian Unlimited* 18 Dec. 2001), have all encouraged a rather emotive debate and demanded changes in the system. These have not produced a new discourse but rather a rehash of the old. Around child protection, the language and bureaucratic expertise is highly political and almost impenetrable, highlighting the inevitable power struggle between the welfare state as 'child protector' and parental rights within the family (Smart 1989).

The social construction of abuse as a problem, alongside the dilemmas of defining sexual abuse, is complicated by the linguistic limitations of the child-protection discourse. For instance, the word *abuse* has become synonymous with child abuse and, in the main, child sexual abuse. The differentiation between types of abuse has become blurred. It is difficult to know how important this lack of difference is in practical terms, except that it is likely to make abuse easier to ignore and minimise by being open to individual subjective interpretation. We have similar difficulties with other descriptive labels such as the term *perpetrator* or *paedophile*, since this label is linked with strangers (usually male), thus allowing incest offending to be ignored (Walklate 2001).

There have been numerous attempts to create better definitions. Hevey and Kenward's contribution was used in the professional guidelines, Working Together (H.M.S.O. 1988), after the Cleveland child-sexual-abuse crisis and was subsequently adopted by the lead child protection agencies, the police, social services, the National Society for the Prevention of Cruelty to Children (NSPCC), health, and education: 'the involvement of dependent, developmentally immature children and adolescents in sexually abusive acts they do not fully comprehend to which they are unable to give informed consent or that violate the social taboos of family roles' (Hevey and Kenward 1989, 210).

There are ambiguities in this definition; for example, the term *sexually abusive acts* was fairly vague and left to those involved with any given case to assess, and terms like *social taboos* and *family roles* gave no real indication of the difficulties within stepfamilies—which may fall outside of the traditional incest framework.

The World Health Organisation (WHO) suggest that there are three elements to consider when defining abuse: first the child, then the abuser, and finally the harm that the abuse may have caused to the victim. The WHO definition is more comprehensive and includes issues of power and trust that are misused to gain control over a child as well as concerns about adult sexual gratification: 'the activity being intended to gratify or satisfy the needs of the other person' (Scottish Executive 2003, part 1, 2).

The other definition we need to consider currently underpins the child-protection policy in England and Wales. It was produced for the new version of Working Together to Safeguard Children 2006 and has utilised the WHO version by including a wide range of contact and noncontact activities.

> Sexual abuse involves forcing or enticing a child or young person to take part in sexual activities, including prostitution, whether or not the child is aware of what is happening. The activities may involve physical contact including penetrative (e.g. rape, buggery or oral sex) or non-penetrative acts. They may include non-contact activities, such as involving children in looking at, or in the production of, pornographic material or watching sexual activities, or encouraging children to behave in sexually inappropriate ways.
>
> (HM Government 2006, 8)

However, this version is not so explicit about adult positions of power, gratification, or family taboos, although these are covered to some degree within the changes in the criminal law discussed below.

A range of subjective interpretations is required of those involved with child protection, whichever definition is taken as a model. So while concerns about child protection are emotive and genuine, working practice may be a balance between professional integrity, life experience, and personal bias.

The Legal Frameworks

Child sexual abuse is rarely a public offence; 'It is more likely to take place in a "private space," where there are rarely witnesses' (Thomas 2000, 12), and for the criminal-justice system this private crime, particularly if it is intrafamilial, can cause difficulties with both obtaining evidence and securing appropriate witnesses to enable any criminal proceedings. In an attempt to establish a protective environment for children, the law has two frameworks within which to act.[4]

The Children Acts

The first course framework concerns the Children Acts (1989 and 2004), which cover noncriminal proceedings within the family courts such as child welfare, parental responsibility, care, and control. Social workers have powers designed to give a legal dimension, through the family courts, to the removal of abused children and those at risk of 'significant harm'[5] to a place of safety. While the Children Acts form a useful focus for decision making, there are a number of issues that can give some cause for concern. In the first instance, 'The question of how responsibility for children's welfare and actions is divided between children, parents and governments remains deeply controversial' (Roberts 2001, 64).

The welfare of children is embedded within the privacy of the family, and this creates dilemmas concerning how much the state should intervene. Even when social workers are involved, there can be conflicts of interest between the promotion of children's welfare and the resolution of family/parental differences, such as following a divorce. These tensions also occur in cases of child protection; keeping families together is part of the underlying philosophy of the Children Acts, and so working with both the parents and the children is crucial but problematic. Furthermore, the philosophy of developing partnerships with parents can be a very difficult one to put into practice where child abuse is suspected. How can professionals build trust and respect with parents when there are questions about the safety of the child? And perhaps the need and desire to keep the family together and work in partnership with parents, particularly mothers, can sometimes render child abuse, and indeed the child, invisible.

Both of the Children Acts (1989, 2004) were built on the philosophical ethos of the United Nations Convention on the Rights of the Child (UNCRC) to which the UK is a signatory. But granting children's rights does not always work out in practice. For instance, children who are 'looked after'[6] still do not have a right to an independent advocate (Roberts 2001); it remains a recommendation. This is a grave concern given the child-abuse disclosures involving foster carers, children's homes, and detention centres. Furthermore, while children are permitted to attend child-protection case conferences, this 'is an exception rather than the rule' (Rendel 2000), which hardly allows them to have their opinions accounted for or even heard within the public forum.

Once any child-protection case reaches the court, however, the Children Acts advocate the appointment of a guardian ad litem.[7] Research (Hunt et al. 1999) suggests that such guardians are appointed in the majority of cases, although the lack of availability unfortunately means that some guardians do not take up appointments until after the initial court cases are heard. These advocates are very important, as our current legal system is not geared towards the appearance of children in courts, a situation unlikely to change in the short term.

> Massive changes in the legal process would also be necessary if children are to participate directly in proceedings. This is extremely rare under the Act. Attendance at hearings even by older children is unusual; some children may not be consulted on the issue and others actively discouraged by practitioners or the judiciary. Research is needed into children's views on this issue. (Hunt et al. 1999)

Despite the fact that evidence for the family courts only needs to be proved as 'the balance of probabilities,' there are still some difficulties in proving harm. So even if cases of child abuse are suspected, there may be delays in implementing emergency procedures. In their review of the research, Hunt, Macleod, and Thomas cite a case where social services suspected a mother of sexually abusing her child but were unable to act.

> We wanted to take proceedings a lot earlier than we did. The solicitor did go to the clerk of the court with the concerns and the clerk took the view that we didn't have enough evidence for an EPO.[8] The social worker was very concerned and rightly (as it turned out) . . . we had to wait for some major blow-up, for the older children to leave home and come to us with their concern. (Hunt et al. 1999)

The recommendations and findings from the Climbie enquiry challenged the child-protection process and were effective in informing some of the new measures outlined in the Children Act 2004. The 2004 act reinforces much of the original philosophy and legislation of 1989, especially in spelling out the joint responsibilities of agencies in working together and sharing information through the common assessment framework and Safeguarding Children Boards.[9] Such changes and additions, along with the appointment of a children's commissioner, are to be applauded, but the full effect of the measures is yet to be assessed.

It is likely that criticisms will continue to be voiced about the Children Acts and the family-court system because decision making remains behind closed doors and works on the principle of the 'balance of probabilities,' which can often leave considerable room for doubt. There are obvious difficulties for professionals, who are frequently performing balancing acts between working with parents and families and ensuring children are protected. Furthermore, the current system offers limited appeal opportunities for parents who stand accused of abusing their children.

The Criminal Law

The second legal framework for child protection is the criminal law, which forms a pathway to prosecute offenders. One of the most difficult dilemmas when facing cases of child sexual abuse is whether or not to invoke criminal proceedings against the perpetrator should there be adequate evidence and suitable child witnesses.[10] Gathering sufficient evidence to take a case to criminal court is difficult in most cases of sexual assault or rape, and forensic clues can be hard to find. This is particularly difficult in the case of child sexual abuse since the victim may disclose a long legacy of assaults rather than a single event that the prosecution case can work on. Furthermore, criminal courts are not child friendly, despite attempts to change.[11] The criminal court is more adversarial and understandably demands a stronger weight of evidence to ensure any convictions will be 'beyond reasonable doubt.' The problems encountered in trying to gain a conviction often have to be balanced against the unpleasant and possibly traumatic experience for the child in the courtroom as well as within the interview and cross-examination process. Pritchard recorded the problems that have been noted by a number of researchers about bringing cases of child sexual abuse, particularly incest, to the criminal courts:

> 'It is readily acknowledged that much within-family sexual abuse is not reported in criminal statistics because of the difficulty of securing a conviction or from an attempt to "spare" the child victims from cross-examination' (Pritchard 2004, 42).

It is the power differential on display in the courtroom that can render the justice process itself as detrimental for the child victim: 'The societal response to detected CSA (child sexual abuse) in the UK (is) at best inadequate and at worst extremely damaging to the children, sometimes mimicking the original abuse dynamics' (Green 2001, 162). The legal complications may indicate that child abuse cases are better conducted within family courts, despite the shortcomings, where evidence of harm or predicted harm is less rigorous and the system slightly more child 'friendly.' Wherever the case is heard, Smart (1989) has commented, the end result can be a no-win situation for child victims.

> It might be useful to consider how we arrived in a situation where child sexual abuse is publicly deplored while the criminal law seems designed

to make it almost impossible to prosecute, or at least to ensure that the child is damaged in the process. (Smart 1989, 51)

Until recently, cases that did reach the criminal court were met by a confusing patchwork and legal labyrinth that had been developed, changed, and added to over the last 150 years. Following a lengthy consultation process,[12] most criminal acts associated with the sexual abuse of children are now covered by the Sexual Offences Act 2003, which has been on the statute book for England and Wales since October 2004 and updates and strengthens the law in a number of ways.

It considers new offences such as sexual grooming,[13] sexual exploitation, encouraging prostitution or pornography, and voyeurism. It recommends some increases in tariffs for offences such as those involving penetration—increased to life if it involves a child under thirteen—and better monitoring of known sex offenders, including registration for offences committed abroad. It offers more recognition to the problems of familial perpetrators by updating the offences and replacing existing gender-specific incest offences relating to sexual activity with children from the family unit. 'It is recognised that the balance of power within the family and the close trusting relationships that exist make children particularly vulnerable to abuse within its environment' (Home Office, 2002, 26 para 58).

Finally, the Sexual Offences Act 2003 confirms the legal age of consent, stating that any sexual activity with someone under sixteen is, even if consent is given, unlawful. Any sexual intercourse with a child under the age of thirteen is assumed to be nonconsensual and charged as rape. Until now it has been comparatively rare to find charges of rape brought to the courts in cases of intrafamilial child sexual abuse (Yates 1990), and more common for the fathers[14] involved to plead guilty to the lesser charge of incest.

Overall, the Sexual Offences Act (2003) has tightened a number of loopholes and incorporated a more appropriate philosophy of child protection into criminal law by taking into account gender, age, and the relationship between offenders and the victims, but whether it serves to protect more children or convict more perpetrators remains to be seen.

Female Offenders and the Legal Process

In general, women are considered to be at low risk of committing criminal offences, and they tend to inflict less harm on their victims (Worrall 1990). So when women are offenders, understanding differences in the underlying gender structures may be important. However, the desire to ensure equivalence relies on 'the premise that sexual categories are factual and symmetrical and that gender is a matter of socialisation' (Worrall 2002, 49).

In the case of child sexual abuse, there are significantly more male than female perpetrators. So it is difficult to consider this offence in a 'gender neutral' way, but the law does attempt to be gender neutral[15] and by doing so is in danger of becoming gender blind. A gender-neutral philosophy fails to account for social structures that create power and the access and control differentials between men and women as well as how 'legal subjects,' whether victims or offenders, are socially constructed (Worrall 1990). The basic problem is that 'gender neutrality is rooted in the idea that both genders, male and female, are equally oppressed' (Rush 1990, 170), leaving women's offending behaviour to be considered in terms of the masculine/male norm—as more malelike (Hudson 2002), as mentally disturbed (Mendel 1995) or as harmless. So, for instance, in the case of sexual abuse there is a persistent 'belief that sexual interactions between older females and juvenile males do not constitute abuse' (Mendel 1995, 30).

Worrall suggests the lack of differential between male and female criminal activity is accounted for within some court processes by invoking a discourse of morality. Of course, this discourse is in itself steeped in gender relations relying on the application of male norms to female behaviour. But she identifies three ways that might be used to explain women's offending behaviour under the umbrella of 'morality' (Worrall 1990).

First, the discourse of domesticity points to the underlying 'factor' that it is male influence that causes female offending. This account serves very well in cases where women are perceived to be following the expected feminine lifestyle and especially if offenders are perceived to be both conventional and good enough mothers. These women are more likely to be seen as victims requiring help and support and as such 'will mitigate their culpability as offenders' (Hudson 2002, 40).

The discourse of sexuality offers a less sympathetic ear to women who are unconventional, seen as unfeminine or childless, and without family. Certain so-called female crimes, such as shoplifting, may be considered 'gender role expressive,' but other crimes—those considered more male, such as violent and sexual crimes—might be less acceptable (Worrall 1990). But men and women's violence can be different, especially cases occurring within intimate relationships, and 'we should not assume that they (women) are acting like men' (Renzetti 1999, 45).

The third discourse Worrall considers is pathological. This is familiar Lombrosian ground, reducing the female offender to biology, not only in terms of being 'sick' but also more importantly by suggesting that women's bodies are predisposed to 'malfunction.' Reducing women in this way has particular significance within the justice process, sometimes encouraging plea bargaining by the defence 'because of the "periodic" nature of her alleged disturbance, it is quite possible for any woman to appear "normal" in the court while claiming that she was "abnormal" at the time of her offence' (Worrall 1990, 64).

Perhaps more importantly, the essentialist view of woman also carries certain notions about the nature of nurturing, motherhood, and femininity that all play a part in our failure to understand women who sexually abuse children. The discourse of pathology comfortably avoids challenging the status quo by reinforcing 'beliefs about the nature of contrariness of women' (Worrall 1990, 64). Rather than attempting a gender-neutral approach, there may be some useful alternative ways to reconsider the analysis of female perpetrators either within a framework of sociocultural forms (Hearn 1988) or by adopting a feminist theory of women's violence (Renzetti 1999).

FAMILY AS A SITE OF ABUSE

A further factor complicating the picture of child sexual abuse in Western societies relates to our stereotypical notion of the family. Part of the reason that the family is so important in the context of abuse is that the sexual abuse usually takes place in private, often between just two people and commonly within a familial setting for the child.

The concept of the family means different things to different people, and there are many types of families: single parent, extended families, single-sex parents, adoptive parents, and foster parents. We need to recognise the wide variety of ethnicity, race, and culture that exists in the UK today. In spite of this, there is an image of the 'ideal type' family, comprising two parents and their children, that is used by government, among others, to establish values, moral standards, average incomes, tax concessions (Roberts 2001), and of course the law. Furthermore, this 'ideal type' family is regarded as the embodiment of a safe private haven for children and adults against the public world of crime and disorder (Saraga 2001). While this perception implies that any danger lurks outside of the family stronghold, the home may not in fact be very safe for small children at all which researchers agree is the real place of danger (Jenks 1996; Saraga 2001; Thorne 1992).

Of course, for most children the family is safe and secure and at least an adequate environment within which to grow and develop. While some families, often single-parent or working-class, are more policed than others, for most, the family remains a private domain and an unregulated space (Duncan 1996). It is this private sanctuary that may act as a blessed retreat to some, but it can also silence children who are trapped behind closed doors. Barrett and McIntosh (1991) have illustrated the problems this isolation can create for women who suffer domestic violence and thus become 'ensnared in a home that may itself become a place of danger for them' (Barrett and McIntosh 1991, 57). Clearly, this is an issue for children as well.

Petra, a survivor of sexual abuse in this study, illustrates the emotions she felt about her family when she described returning home each day from school: ' . . . you had to go home . . . in the evening you had to go home. It was like having a big stone in your stomach every day of your life . . . outside I was a happy child. The covering up was very good . . . ' (Petra).

Petra did not disclose the abuse she suffered until she was in her thirties and she found it a situation from which it was very difficult to disengage.

On the face of it, we might question how the abused child and abusive family go unnoticed. This omission may be wrapped up in the visions of the ideal family life. Gittens (1998) has pointed out, there is a considerable difference between what we may perceive the family should be and how people really live their lives, a point emphasised by some of the survivors interviewed for this research:

> . . . things would have looked OK. We had a car; we had a TV; we went on holiday . . . on Sunday we would have Sunday lunch and the tea would be put on a trolley . . . we did a lot of entertaining. . . . (Alice)

> . . . the family were seen by outsiders as loving and affectionate. . . . (Celia)

> . . . there was the abuse side, the horrendous emotional blackmail and that side to it. But then on the other side we were very much an upper middle class family. All my clothes were handmade . . . I went to ballet school and private school and all sorts of things like that. The outer side was very upper middle class and yet all the horrible stuff was going on underneath. (Penny)

Despite all its shortcomings, the concept of the ideal family has enormous appeal. The emotional security the family appears to offer and the opportunity to produce and raise children are compounded by the idea that it is seen as the natural thing to do. It is the public popularity of the family situation that makes it difficult to critique or indeed to deconstruct. The family is perceived as 'naturally given and as socially and morally desirable' (Barrett and McIntosh 1991, 26), and it is these essentialist overtones that create some problems for understanding and identifying child abuse. They inhibit us from taking a more public look at the site of the family and from challenging parental behaviour. There can be no accountability if the doors are permanently closed.

Even when sexual abuse is revealed, we have a further dilemma when we have to align our concept of the family with the notion that some known adult, possibly the parent, is the perpetrator. Saraga has suggested that this problem is sometimes 'resolved by constructing two types of family, normal harmonious families and dysfunctional or problem families' (2001, 231) within which abuse occurs. But this division really only accounts for some abusive families and tends to focus on those who are easy to police. Consequently, there is a constant tension between any public support for the family as the ideal, safe, child-rearing site requiring privacy and the demands for state intervention to protect children. We can recognise this within some of the accounts of the professionals.[16] These problems are exacerbated because parental authority within most families is endorsed by the state (Donzelot 1980), and parental control is assumed to be a key role in the moral upbringing of children. Thus, there has been a sense of reluctance to make any strong links between child abuse, the family, and punishment or retribution (Saraga 2001). Although Saraga's suggestion refers mainly to physical child abuse, we have been as slow to encourage appropriate punishment and protection in connection with the sexual abuse that occurs in families. The few notable exceptions have been cases that have created uproar and demanded a renegotiation of parental rights.[17]

Some of the difficulties the professionals identified when dealing with female sexual abusers were related to these stereotypical ideas of the family structure. So what are the alternative ways to view the family? Challenges to the original, often rather functional, discourse on the family can be identified in the work of Giddens (1992), who considers intimate and familial relationships, and in the work of Morgan (1996), who follows this theme in his discussion about carers and caring and his concept of 'family practices' rather than family units. Of course, theory often finds difficulty in challenging our stereotypes, but if we are to find new formats for protecting children, we need to develop new ways of understanding the family and family relationships.

Smart and Neale (1999) point to Beck and Beck-Gernsheim's (1995) analysis of intimate family relationships suggesting that the focus of the adult has changed. The love of the child has become an important new factor affecting changing intimate relationships. In other words, when love within a partnership fails, the love from children remains, so as adult relationships become less reliable, children become the centre of permanence and satisfaction. The child has become precious and irreplaceable in this late modern society. 'The more other relationships become interchangeable and revocable, the more a child can become the focus of new hopes—it is the ultimate guarantee of permanence, providing an anchor for one's life' (Beck and Beck-Gernsheim 1995, 73).

This does not guarantee protection from abuse and may further isolate the child; therefore, children need to be empowered in some way so that they feel able to expose child abuse. This is a difficult issue that not only encroaches on the power and control of parents but also treads a fine line between the protection of children within a paradigm of welfarism and granting children citizenship rights. We will discuss this dilemma later in the chapter on the victims of abuse; suffice it to say here that the tensions between child protection and children's rights are problematic. As Kitzinger (1988) summaries,

> despite some encouraging individual aspects of the contemporary child protection movement, the mainstream campaigns conspicuously fail to take any overall stand against the structural oppression of children.

They are, therefore, not only severely limited in what they can achieve, but they also often reinforce the very ideologies, which expose children to exploitation in the first place. (Kitzinger 1988, 85)

MOTHERS, MOTHERING, AND SEXUALITY

Apart from our belief in the family as a cohesive and natural unit, some of the confusion about women who sexually abuse children is linked to the homogenised notion of masculinity and femininity and womanhood. Assuming these concepts are stable is to misunderstand the influence of social structures and the analysis of differentiation and individualism (Liddle 1993). However, all women, whether mothers or not, are socially constructed in terms of the maternal, and because of this they are assumed to share the universal nurturing role: 'Woman is conflated with mother, and together appears as an undifferentiated and unchanging monolith.' (Glenn 1994, 13).

Rich (1978) has suggested others have defined women with titles such as mother, matron, old maid. In other words, woman has been defined according to her relationship to maternity (Lawler 1996). There have been some moves towards change for women in the world of education and work. But within many households it is the man's wage that remains the economic key, and ultimately it is the woman who takes responsibility for the children, even though the care may be to some extent shared (Segal 1995).

Women are presumed to have a special relationship with children, particularly their own, that is fully endorsed by society, and it is this liberty, combined with our desexualised image of the mother figure, that hides the female sexual abuser: 'The expectations of the female role simultaneously expects a degree of bodily experience between woman and child and denies the existence of sexuality in women' (Plummer 1981, 228).

The expectation of a close, loving bond between mother and child gives women a licence to be intimate; it also means that their motives are generally interpreted as benign. In the adult world, such close physical relationships are rarely without a sexual dimension, but women as mothers are expected to be asexual. The binary expectations of women are thus highlighted by motherhood, which is a role set apart from female sexuality: 'The virgin or the whore, the pure or the impure, the nurturer or the seducer is either the asexual mother or the sexualised beauty, but one precludes the other' (Young 1990, 196).

The mother is positioned in a sexual paradox. Her sexuality is presumed suppressed by her maternity, and sometimes this sexual enigma conceals the reality of the relationship. Banning suggests, 'Mothers are perceived as nurturing and asexual to their children . . . at worst their behaviour is labelled as seductive . . . not harmful. The same behaviour in a father is labelled child molestation' (Banning 1989, 567).

In this way the asexual mother could be seen as a mythical creation of social convenience. Young (1990) encapsulates the ultimate in infant care, which in other circumstances would be identified at least as sensual if not overtly sexual. Breast feeding can be highlighted as one of the most significant features in the social desexualisation of the mother; the act of breast feeding is considered an asexual act. Mothers are presumed to be givers not takers; therefore, gaining any sensual pleasure from nurturing creates a paradox between the mother myth and the sexual whore that cannot be socially tolerated.

Sexual competition between fathers and their children is quashed by desexualising motherhood because it ensures that mothers remain dependent upon men for sexual pleasure (Young 1990). The patriarchal rule of power and control has determined the agenda of social roles and encouraged a strong emphasis on incest taboos. These taboos are so significant that they are embedded deep in our unconscious, either through a subliminal social process or, as Freudians suggest, as part of the oedipal complex. The implication here for female sexuality is that the sensual function of the breast must be suppressed for nursing mothers. Here we have an uncomfortable paradox because acceptance of this version of events means we can ignore, deny, and mislabel oversexualised behaviour between mothers and their infants. Yet the breast-feeding experience can enhance a close, loving mother-infant bond. While it may not be relevant to ponder on this conundrum, what is important in terms of female sexual abusers is that these ambiguous notions regarding mothers and mothering exist. Given this ambiguity, it is hardly surprising that, for some, the prescribed role between mother and sexual being gets confused.

So who is the ideal mother?

> She must be completely devoted not just to her children, but to her role. She must be the mother who understands her children, who is all-loving and . . . all-giving. She must be capable of enormous sacrifice. She must be fertile and possess maternal drives, unless she is unmarried and/or poor, in which case she will be vilified for precisely the same things . . . she must embody all the qualities traditionally associated with femininity such as nurturing, intimacy and softness. That's how we want her to be. That's how we intend to make her. (Forna 1998, 3)

The mythical stereotype of the good mother is promoted by both the media and the criminal-justice system. According to Smart (1995), the norms and expectations of mothering and motherhood were established as a result of the notion of dangerous mothers and the infanticide laws of the seventeenth century. The media have helped to reinforce our conception of good mothers, bad mothers, and dangerous mothers by contrasting stories of the perfect mother, dying for the sake of her child, alongside the war against young single mothers and mothers who continue to work or take risks with drugs, alcohol, or lifestyles (Forna 1998).

Smart suggests that the key to understanding motherhood lies with the single mother who is treated by the law and society alike as 'problematic and destabilising' (Smart 1995, 197). All of these ideas are established and reinforced by the various developmental theories of childhood, including and especially psychological approaches.

> Theoretical formulations of infant development systematically blame and devalue women as mothers . . . they (mothers) are expected to provide a hyper-sensitive interactive partner for the young baby, a partner who is at the same time natural, educationally constructive (but non-directive), and who must at all costs enjoy what she is doing. Mothers must fall in love with their babies as well as serving them. (Morss 1996, 145)

Modern changes towards a romanticised maternity have made it appear easy and natural, disallowing any ambivalent feelings that may occur (Coward 1997), and the social idealisation and glorification of motherhood has allowed us to ignore female perversity (Welldon 1988). But the overglorification of motherhood has several other effects. The myth of the ideal natural mother creates problems for those whose mothering is not considered 'good enough.'[18] Their behaviour may be cast as 'unfeminine,' and the sense of failure brings with it confusion and guilt. One mother who sexually abused both of her children found confronting the facts of her 'failures' too painful. This was made considerably worse by memories of her own childhood abuse and the removal of her children into local authority care. ' . . . the mother at the end of the care proceedings had been persuaded to allow police to investigate allegations of abuse on her . . . the day before she was due to give a police interview she killed herself.' (family lawyer).

Professionals also use the myth of motherhood to assume a 'natural' instinct for women to become at least 'good enough' mothers. But as Smart has highlighted, the heavy policing by health and social welfare agencies would suggest that 'motherhood is not a natural condition' (Smart 1996, 37). The normalising of motherhood enables an institution to develop a set of parameters about 'good mothering' that can be used for assessment and control. In this way, the high expectations that professionals had of the mothering role, 'the good mother was no longer simply the one who fed and cleansed properly, she would be inadequate if she failed to love properly and to express this love in the correct fashion' (Smart 1996, 44). Consequently, there are high demands upon mothers who may suffer 'an increased potential for maternal failure' (Gordon 1992, 274).

Carlen (1990) noted that probation officers were inclined to promote the good mothering and housewifery abilities of their clients in court, recognising that this was beneficial for judiciary decision making and outcomes.[19] Such a technique may be useful for some female defendants, but by reinforcing so-called norms, convicted women become stereotyped as other. Mothers may feel failures if they are unable to reach the high standards of excellence set by agencies. This was a problem highlighted by one abuser in this study. 'Once I had Richard I knew I wasn't capable of looking after children . . . basically no mothering instincts' (Janet). During her second pregnancy, Janet suggests she was in total denial. ' . . . all the way through pregnancy . . . I kept saying, I'm not pregnant' (Janet).

On face value, these comments appeared to indicate that Janet recognised her lack of mothering skills and also perhaps her lack of desire to be a mother. Of course, many mothers feel failures for all sorts of reasons, and some mothers feel deskilled when it comes to child care. Most of them do not go on to abuse their children. But perhaps we should be offering more support to mothers to develop childcare skills as well as to acknowledge and enable them to overcome any fears or concerns. By demanding the ideal type of mother and indeed the ideal type of responsive child, we offer abusers an ideal type of rationale . . . 'I can't do it . . . I'm not cut out to be a mother . . . .' So, by presuming women are natural mothers and by maintaining an image of what it is to be a mother, we not only create feelings of discontent, failure, and guilt, but we collude with some abusive mothers by excusing their behaviour as lack of ability. While we are continuing to consider mothering from an essentialist perspective, we are left in a paradox. Essentialism allows us 'absolution from responsibility,' allows us to justify the unacceptable and claim 'natural' as a defence (Young 1999, 103).

Wilczynski (1995), in her research into filicides, identified two categories that could be relevant to our discussion here. She labelled one of the motivations as 'the unwanted child.' These killings were most commonly committed by women who were described as passive and immature and who denied or concealed their pregnancies. This might make us question Janet's relationship with her daughter. The second category is 'the secondary altruistic filicide.' Again, these killings are mainly committed by mothers and are sometimes linked to depression, the cause of which is not always clear.

> These women expressed acute feelings of failure to measure up to society's standards of 'good' mothers or wives. For instance, one woman regarded herself as a bad mother and wife, worried that the child was abnormal in some way, and felt that she did everything but it was never enough. (Wilczynski 1995, 170)

These findings give us an insight into how important the social stereotypes of mothers and mothering are and the response from some women who may be told or who perceive their skills as 'inadequate.' Such women are not just excluded from the 'good enough' mother club but may lack the social capital to over come or challenge the labelling.

Motherhood has been recognised as one of the most high-pressured jobs (Coward 1997), which is made much more difficult because, as a 'natural instinct,' it is unrecognised and unrewarded. This does take its toll. When discussing mothers who murder, Coward concluded that 'lack of social support gave them no way out of their crazy decisions' (1997, 115). Maybe this applies to other abuse because we set impossible targets and ideals for mothering and motherhood and we offer an insufficient support system, even when mothers admit lack of bonding and child-care skills (Welldon 1988).

In other instances, it is the image we have created of the 'mother' that confuses professionals involved in child protection, as the sexual abuse of children by women maybe disguised as child care. This study would suggest that for the actors involved with the abuse, there is no confusion. Female perpetrators who understand the expectations of their roles are able to hide behaviour that has sexual meanings within the ordinary and everyday. Such sexualised behaviour is often recognised by the victims but may go unobserved by onlookers or is minimised as overenthusiastic child care or maybe excused as an exceptionally strong 'mother-love' bond.

A discussion of mothering in connection with female perpetrators needs to include some comments concerning maternal ambivalence. Maybe this concept explains some of the problems experienced by mothers who sexually abuse their children. Understanding the love-hate relationship that mothers have for their children moves us away from the discourse of 'natural' mothering and the disappointments and guilt experienced when that maternal relationship appears to fail (Featherstone 2004). Part of the difficulty for women who abuse is the misunderstanding of their own feelings and the misinterpretation of the behaviour of their children. When maternal ambivalence is manageable, the internal conflict between love and hate motivates mothers into understanding their children and their own feelings. Problems can arise when the ambivalent state is unmanageable because then the 'potential for ambivalence to foster thought and spark concern is overwhelmed by the anxiety generated when hate no longer feels mitigated by love' (Parker 1997, 22).

Any mother who dares to display ambivalent feelings towards her child may retreat shamefaced and alone and may also experience extra policing and criticism by welfare agencies. Welldon (1988) found that women who sought help for their 'shortcomings' or ambivalent feelings were often ignored: 'People simply don't want to know. I see women who have been to all kinds of agencies to try and get help and they are simply not taken seriously' (Welldon, quoted in Search 1988, 83).

So even those mothers who are prepared to publicly recognise the paradoxical and tenuous bond they have with their child have their behaviour minimised and denied. It may be that part of the reason for this is that it is more comfortable to imagine that all mothers love their children 'or if they do not they can be helped to do so' (Featherstone 1997, 186). I would argue that it is important to allow mothers to express their concerns and understand their feelings and frustrations because misunderstanding the maternal love-hate feelings may create motives and rationale for abuse. The silence that surrounds the paradoxical feelings mothers have for their children is a problem as it results in 'abnormal' maternal reactions and relationships being 'pathologised.' For example, Young suggested that in order to understand postnatal depression we need to challenge pathological approach and to develop 'a less sentimental approach to motherhood [that]could allow women safe expression of their negative feelings towards small children' (Young 1993, 119).

We have created a social stereotype, the mother who is expected to nurture and love her children without question, and it is this very idea that leaves us with the dilemma. For how can women who feel differently disclose concerns without being patronisingly reassured or misunderstood? We need to avoid assumptions about identity and maternity and allow women space to tell their story. 'Understanding the female sexual offender requires the capacity to suspend stereotypes about "maternal instincts" and the ability to hear, from the offender herself, the story of her own mothering' (Motz 2001, 57).

Furthermore, our idealisation of mothers has made it more difficult for child victims to speak out and can accentuate the fantasy of the all-powerful omnipotent mother (Featherstone 1997). In a social world that upholds images of women as nurturers and carers, how can child victims find and approach adults to whom they can disclose? What words can they use to talk about the abuse? How can you disclose sexual abuse by your mother? Clearly, for some victims disclosure is very difficult and for others impossible. Sgroi and Sargent (1993) have described the dilemma that may be faced by these child victims:

> It simply may generate too much cognitive dissonance for . . . (survivors) . . . to acknowledge to self or to others that he or she was sexually abused by her or his mother. In other words, to view oneself as so powerful a sexual object that 'my own mother succumbed to the temptation to have sexual contact with me,' may be a belief that is too threatening and overwhelming for the child to integrate and absorb. (Sgroi and Sargent 1993, 24)

Our perception of motherhood is not isolated but part of a late modern capitalist society that privileges certain ideal social structures and social identities on the one hand and condemns those who fail to conform on the other. Imposing ideological expectations on women who are mothers can lead to anger, frustration, and resentment. 'These negative feelings sometimes lead to behaviour that is less than maternal' (Glenn 1994, 10).

The child victims of maternal incest have to disillusion the social world by shaking motherhood from its pedestal and at the same time risk permanent loss of the primary maternal attachment.

FEMINIST PERSPECTIVES

In the final section of this chapter, I want to look at the underlying influence of the dominant feminist theory of child sexual abuse. While recognising there is any number of feminisms at any one time, there has been a general underlying agreement amongst feminists that sexual violence is male (Walklate 2001). In other words, acts of violence such as rape, domestic violence, and child sexual abuse are perpetrated by men on women or young girls (Bryson 1999; Walklate 2001). The differences between feminist perspectives relating to the issue of male violence have been concerning its location. For instance, Walklate (2001) suggested the liberal feminists might locate male violence in a few 'sick' or 'perverted' men, suggesting that such a crime, while a reflection of masculinity, is limited to those who are outside of the norm and that socialist feminists describe sexual violence in terms of the capitalist system by explaining that the inequality of capitalism creates frustration that may lead to male violence. But it is the early radical feminist theory relating to sexual violence that has dominated the field, placing male violence firmly within the realms of male power and masculinity viewed in relation to normative masculine gendered practice (Cossins 2000). Such an approach clearly raises difficulties with the exposure of female abusers and any analysis of their behaviour and also creates paradoxical tensions for feminists when faced with the reality of female perpetrators.

The radical feminist hypothesis evolved in the wake of the second phase of feminism in the 1970s and 1980s. The development of this approach was twofold. There was a commitment from political activists to not only raise the profile of women but to deal with social issues that had until this point largely been ignored. The concerns raised were centred on the family and patriarchal power and included domestic violence, child sexual abuse, including incest, and rape. At the same time, academic feminists (Brownmiller 1981; Dworkin 1981; Kelly 1988; Stanko 1985) were creating a significant feminist critique of the contemporary theoretical and methodological paradigms available within the social sciences. The two-pronged attack challenged the establishment's persistence in maintaining patriarchy and suggested that power structures, especially within the family, had been ignored (Dworkin 1981; Kelly 1988).

One of the dramatic changes in the traditional sociological view was created by feminists who identified incest as a social problem. This was a profound theoretical shift in the way in 'which incest was conceived in the sociological imagination' (Bell 1993, 3). Feminists (Kelly 1988; Worrall 1990) suggested that explanations of child sexual abuse needed a better understanding of power relationships within families and an analysis of the lived experiences of women. It is interesting to note that there was little actual analysis of these power structures (Bell 1993); rather, there was an assumption that all men have power, and women and children do not. While ignoring the existence of the lone female sexual abuser, many feminists did not deny the collusive mother existed but chose to analyse these women in terms of masculinity and power by suggesting that 'maternal collusion in incest, when it occurs, is a measure of maternal powerlessness' (Herman 1981, cited in Waldby 1989, 100). It is the very strong emphasis on masculinity and power, rooted in the patriarchal discourse, that limits the scope for explanations of female perpetrators.

As far as female perpetrators are concerned, there were two main problems to the radical approach to child sexual abuse.

The first was that it assumes an essentialist discourse by suggesting that nearly all men are aggressive and nearly all women are victims (Allen 1990; Carrington 2002; Hudson 2002; Mendel 1995), and within this setting it is difficult to perceive women as perpetrators. The essentialist stance infers that women are responsible for avoiding their own victimisation given that 'men can't avoid their destiny as potential rapists' (Carrington 2002, 131), a position that further encourages the depiction of women as passive and nonabusing.

The second problem is that explaining sexual violence as a result of masculinity and male power is too reductionist: It proposes a simple solution to a complex event (Walklate 2001). Child sexual abuse needs a much broader framework not only to account for the difference between genders but also for different masculinities and femininities. We need to include some analysis about the way in which sociocultural forms condone abuse and the context of the abusive behaviour itself. Furthermore, we need to account for the fact that power is not just related to patriarchy and gender but is linked to other social concepts such as class, race, and sexuality (O'Dell 2003; Reavey and Warner 2003).

Despite the problems within the feminist analysis, there are some ways it can be used to consider lone female abusers. For instance, if we assume that women's incestuous desires are inhibited by social conditioning and role norms, then we can expect the situation to be challenged by encouraging gender equality. Banning (1989) argued this point and suggested that feminism itself, by seeking and demanding a change in the status quo, is capable of creating a 'masculinised' woman—a woman seeking power for herself, designing and desiring a new image of femininity, no longer the passive victim. Banning raised the question, 'Could it be that in this struggle, those women for whom power is very important but who feel insecure, inadequate and dis-empowered, may be predisposed to sexually abuse children, if other predisposing factors exist?' (Banning 1989, 568).

In other words, Banning is suggesting that male and female incest perpetrators can both be analysed using the theory of masculinised power.

This is a tempting explanation and could be useful for understanding some female abusers. There is a movement of power within family units (Gordon 1992), and comparatively powerless women potentially have control within the family, particularly over their children (Ong 1986). After all, while there may be a definable, structural powerlessness amongst women, especially those who are mothers, in the public sphere this may turn into 'one of total power as a mother in the private sphere' (Wolfers 1993, 100). The distribution of power within the family is indeed asymmetric, but this asymmetry drifts between the subjects, creating a constant variety of hierarchies. Although utilising familial hierarchies of power maybe useful ways to control and manipulate victims (Finkelhor 1983), power should not be used as the only explanation of incest. 'The commission of incest can have the effect of disempowering the child. . . . (but) the need for power over the child is not the primary motivation for the act of incest' (Cossins 2000, 59).

The feminist approach has not only suggested that incest is masculine and predatory but that it is heterosexual (Walklate 2001). For many years this notion created a problem for boys who were sexually abused by male adults. Whilst this remains controversial enough, mother-daughter incest is still battling to find a way into the discourse (Rosencrans 1997). It could be argued that as far as child sexual abuse is concerned, the feminist discourse has prioritised heterosexuality so that male perpetrators have become normalised. Paternal incest is considered exaggerated naturalism because, socially, masculinity and paternity require the attributes of protection, power, possession, and passion. So male sexual offenders can readily be rationalised in terms of their sexuality (Smart 1989). However, such explanations do not apply to the female sexual abuser, whose sexuality is often replaced with pathology. The way that female sexuality and motherhood are constructed removes sexual abuse by women outside the continuum of expected female behaviour. Women are assumed to be less likely to be predatory and more likely to respect the individual nature of children. 'In short, incestuous behaviour on the part of the mother is not discursively incited in the same way that it is for men' (Bell 1993, 123).

Attempting to even discuss, let alone research and analyse, female abusers has been fiercely opposed by some women's groups as antifeminist. For instance, there was a serious attempt by some feminists to thwart the first national conference on female sexual abuse held by Kidscape in London in 1992. There is an uncomfortable paradox here, for while there are statistically far more male sexual offenders than female, we risk all we have uncovered about child sexual abuse by confirming the existence of the 'unpathologised' female perpetrator. Understandably, for some feminists, this concept is perhaps too painful to contemplate.

Russell, who has written considerably on the subject of child sexual abuse, minimised the reporting of female perpetrators as a defence against feminist arguments by claiming: 'We believe that some workers and researchers are ideologically uncomfortable with the idea of a male preponderance and thus have been quick to rush to the possibility that it might not be true' (Russell 1984, 184).

In no way does Russell presume that there are no female perpetrators, but like many feminists during this period she felt that any research, other than claims to the extraordinary and pathological nature of such women, deflected from the main culprits of child sexual abuse. And it is not difficult to see her point. Forbes (1992) was also concerned about the investigation of female sexual abusers, suggesting that within a male-dominated society it offered 'an ideological retreat for some professionals and policy makers' (Forbes 1992, 109).

On the positive side, the feminist discourse has moved us away from the mother blaming adopted by other approaches, such as the family systems theory and psychoanalysis (Cossins 2000). It challenges any notion of placing the responsibility for abuse on the 'sexually precocious' child (McKinnon 1995) by perceiving the problems as one of normal masculine aggression (Bryson 1999). 'Although it is important to acknowledge that women do abuse sexually, the evidence would suggest that there may be systematic features of masculine sexuality that contribute to sexual abuse' (Featherstone 2004, 123).

It was also the feminists (Kelly 1988, 1997a) who challenged the concept of the cycle of abuse, which is difficult to align with the fact that most child victims are female and the majority of perpetrators are male. But by taking the 'conventional' feminist route, we are faced with a perspective that is dominated by ideas of masculinity and power; and by assuming a male power and a female subservience, we are in danger of adopting a deterministic stance that encourages a notion of inevitability and constancy. A cross-gendered phenomenon such as child sexual abuse needs a closer consideration and analysis to develop new theoretical approaches; otherwise we can only consider female sexual abusers as psychotics or as male coerced or as masculinised and thus deny them any agency, however limited that might be.

Smart (1995) has clearly summarised the difficulties:

> The problem with formulating sexual abuse as an outcome of masculine sexuality has been the denial of sexual abuse by women. The location of 'bad' sexuality with the homogeneous masculine has meant that women have been denied any responsibility for their harmful behaviour. Women's (sexual) violence has perhaps been feminism's 'best kept secret' and we need to develop further the means of analysing it rather than denying it. (Smart 1995, 113)

As the above quote indicates, there are new debates emerging from the feminist discourses about women as violent offenders (Carlen 2002; Carrington 2002; Hudson 2002; Worrall 2002).

Hearn (1988) has developed a framework for understanding child sexual abuse including an in-depth consideration of masculinity and violence through a deconstruction of masculinities and the sociocultural forms that condone sexually aggressive behaviour. The framework takes us onto a different pathway and away from the risk and individualistic dangerousness models towards explanations as to why some men offend and not others (Walklate 2001). It also has something to offer in the analysis of female offenders in terms of developing rationales and social acceptance through sociocultural forms.

Renzetti's (1999) work offers us some further ideas, utilising what theories we do have and making suggestions for extending this analysis. She suggests that the feminist analysis may suffice in some instances of female sexual offenders, but not all women, or indeed all circumstances, are the same: 'The fact is that women use violence in a variety of contexts and relationships: women may abuse their children, their parents and . . . their intimate partners' (Renzetti 1999, 47).

Furthermore, we need to be sure that gender remains prominent in the analysis of female violence and not assume that women are acting like men. This means avoiding a gender-neutral approach, especially to criminal justice, since this decontextualises women's violence and considers it 'in terms of a male normative standard juxtaposed against stereotypes of respectable femininity' (Renzetti 1999, 49).

Renzetti offers new possibilities, less formulated than Hearn, but nevertheless a very valuable contribution by considering ways to build a feminist theory of female violence. First, it needs to contextualise women's use of violence: what does it mean to them, and how do they experience the behaviour? Second, the research needs to be collaborative or at least take into account several viewpoints. There is no one way of seeing and understanding or indeed analysing this behaviour. So it requires that academics, offenders, survivors, and practitioners are all involved. Finally, feminists need to take ownership of the problem if they are to avoid criticism and backlash (Kelly 1996; Renzetti 1999). It is important to understand that 'documenting, denouncing and acting to prevent men's violence against women do not require us to deny women's agency' (Renzetti 1999, 52).

We are only beginning to challenge traditional approaches, and it remains difficult to work outside the dominant feminist approach to child sexual abuse. This is partly because feminist explanations of sexual violence have merged into social 'folklore,' as indicated by the rationale of the interviewees involved in this project.

CONCLUSION

What emerges in this general contextualising chapter is the widespread assumption that women do not sexually abuse children, or at least not of their own volition. We have difficulty in identifying and defining sexually abusive experiences. But we assume a male offender since this aligns with notions of masculinity and gender bias within the popular child-sexual-abuse discourse. I have tried to construct an understanding of child sexual abuse in which we can place the female sexual abuser and the associated tensions to form the framework for the analytic chapters that follow.

The professionals clearly have dilemmas when faced with female abusers not just in dealing with family issues and those interpersonal relationships but also with the stereotypical notions of the ideal mother and constraints of the current child-protection system. Child victims recognise their sense of powerlessness within the abusive situation, and the popular image of mothers as naturally nurturing can silence their voices. We should continue to work towards developing a discourse that allows children some empowerment through citizenship rights.

Women in our society remain the primary carers, and, partly because of this role, they are given permission to 'be physical' with children in a way that is generally excluded to men. The challenge to understand sexual abuse by women is embroiled in the passivity of femininity and desexualisation of mothers and mothering. By the creation of an asexual child carer, we have surrounded mother and child with a mythical cloak of security and love. We ignore any notion of sexual expression or desire within that relationship. Both mother and child are hidden from society. The woman has our permission to be an all-powerful mother and her child is dependent upon her. We are still finding our way as far as the female perpetrator is concerned. However, the realisation of the ambiguous feelings that mothers have for their children feeds into some of our understanding of female sexual abusers, and maybe we can develop this theme to explain some of their 'unfeminine' behaviour.

Underlying all of these discussions has been the feminist discourse. It has been very dominant in terms of child sexual abuse and has laid the foundations for social definitions and explanations, but it does little towards considering causation in terms of female sexual abusers. If this is the case, then maybe we need to change our focus for male perpetrators as well. We are only at the very beginning of a long and difficult process. But by analysing the stories of female perpetrators from a variety of sources and perspectives, we can start to identify how, and if, there are any themes that challenge our current understanding of child sexual abuse.

3   The Professionals

> We can . . . no longer disregard the fact that children can be and
> are both physically and sexually abused by the very adults who are
> responsible for their care . . . and in confronting that reality, it be-
> comes necessary to move beyond the assumption that a simple re-
> liance on adults to promote the well-being of children . . . is an
> adequate approach to caring for children. (Lansdown 2001, 89)

Thus, we have developed a child protection system within a range of
agencies. But even so, professionals face significant difficulties and dilemmas, especially when dealing with cases of child sexual abuse, more so
if the perpetrator is female. The problems that they face are constantly
evolving.

> Problems rise and fall . . . depending on such intertwined factors as
> demographic changes, shifting gender expectations, economic strains
> and racial conflicts . . . Any given concept of childhood or the dan-
> gers that children face cannot be understood without reference to
> these shifting foundations. (Jenkins 1998, 216)

The issues highlighted in this chapter not only relate to complications
that child-protection workers have in carrying out their tasks but also
reveal the assumptions they make, often hidden within their own child-
protection discourse.

   The difficulties of agencies working together have been well documented
and demonstrate that each agency carries a distinct agenda, from child
protection to prosecution of the offender (Payne 2000; Witz 1992).
Despite the mutual desire to protect children, there is often an underlying
disharmony in multiagency work concerning the focus and intent, which
can bias decisions and opinions. Furthermore, since all those involved with
child protection have something to gain (Jenkins 1998)—for instance,
social workers weaving careers; police gaining resources; religious groups
strengthening moral codes and family values—decision making may

present personal dilemmas on occasions. The variety of perspectives involved can also reflect on the relationship that professionals develop with the offender, the victim, or indeed with other agencies. The policy of child-protection agencies remains one of working together, but, as the example below shows, it is not always reflected in practice.

> . . . the health visitor who was assigned the task of monitoring the family pursued her own line. 'He fell over a little while ago and blackened his eye,' the mother confided to the researcher. The health visitor said, 'Don't let the social worker see it! Put a plaster on it if she comes, or hide it! She's like a Mum to me!' (Packman and Randall 1989, 104)

There are some differences in the way professionals practice when they come into contact with females who sexually abuse children. On these occasions, child protection workers tend to exclude or minimise the abusive behaviour. Professional denial has been recorded in other research (Denov 2004; Hetherton and Beardsall 1998; Welldon 1988) and appears to be linked to social structures such as the family, female sexuality, and the essential nature of woman.

When the evidence of female perpetrators is overwhelming, professionals face a paucity of services and resources to offer either the offender or the victim, and they may lack the expertise to put any action into practice. Of course, there is a limit on services available for the male perpetrator as well, and this is also a problem. However, child protection initiatives, especially in cases of child sexual abuse, have traditionally relied upon the protecting mother to house and comfort the victim and police the unconvicted male perpetrator. In cases where there is a female offender, identifying a protecting environment for the child is more problematic.

PROFESSIONAL BOUNDARIES AND BARRIERS

Before we consider some of the ways that the sexually abusive behaviour of women can be rationalised, we need to highlight three barriers relating to professional practice.

Roles and Values

The first barrier, which challenges competent and cooperative multidisciplinary working, could be attributed to the different values and perception generated within the professions. As suggested above, each of the key organisations generally has a distinct focus, which forms a working goal. It may be difficult sometimes to collaborate fully in child-protection work while aims are so variable; any lack of understanding and communication can have disastrous results. For instance, there was considerable lack of communication between professionals in the case of Victoria Climbie, and the subsequent enquiry condemned the failure of professionals to work together (Laming 2003). Despite the clear intent of individual workers from all the agencies involved to protect children, and a duty of collaboration imposed by the Children Acts 1989 and 2004, there seem to be several threads that lead to problems with sharing information and collaborative working.

Clearly, the focus individuals have within any organisation has a part to play. Social workers have the main statutory role and responsibility for child protection. The police retain a more investigative role that works towards prosecution of the offender and protection of the public, although they do have a very clear remit of child protection within the Children Acts. These two agencies have to work particularly closely during the investigative stage of any child-protection proceedings. Professionals working in health and education have a slightly different focus. It is often referrals from these workers that initially raise concern about individual children, and any diagnosis delivered by health professionals may determine the course of action to be taken.

For example, it was the medical examination concerning the ambiguous diagnosis of anal dilation that determined which children were removed from home diagnosed as having been sexually abused in the Cleveland affair (DHSS, 1988). And it was the misdiagnosis of scabies that created a problem for professionals in the Victoria Climbie case (Laming 2003). As a result of numerous enquiries, the recommendation of further training and more effective working together, particularly in complicated cases of child protection, has been seen as the answer to professional failure (Sinclair and Bullock 2002). However, such a process does not account for any professional closure[1] (Witz 1992), which may occur if workers, or organisations, feel that their expertise is under threat or when resources are limited (Morrison 1997).

Payne (2000) suggests that team working is itself a paradox. Building multidisciplinary relationships with other agencies may mean that professionals are more obsessed and possessive about their own work and behaviour. For instance, managers often see interagency working as an 'instrument for carrying out the organisations' objectives' (Payne 2000, 1). Furthermore, the concentration of focus on individual performance, the team building and the organisational objectives, may exclude service users from any involvement, despite the political move towards partnerships.

Barrett (1996), while discussing multidisciplinary teamwork in the mental health setting, points out that professions have developed policies and protocols over the years to maintain distinction and difference. He suggests that the ownership of specialist knowledge is important for both individual status and professional boundaries. The notion of ownership of knowledge flies in the face of multidisciplinary cooperation and collaboration. While each child protection worker may be usefully adding a unique perspective in cases of child sexual abuse, within the struggles for autonomy the concept of working together can be lost.

However, there does not appear to be the same struggle for professional autonomy suggested by other work (Barrett 1996; Witz 1992) and child protection inquiries (DHSS 1988; Laming 2003) when women are the offenders. Perhaps part of the reason is due to the gender of the perpetrator, as illustrated in the work of Hetherton and Beardsall (1998).

In the first instance, their research shows that cases of women who sexually abuse children 'may be less likely to be acted on than if the abuse was perpetrated by a male' (Hetherton and Beardsall 1998, 1279).[2] Female perpetrators are likely to have their behaviour adjusted to fit feminine stereotypes—such as overenthusiastic childcare—to be masculinised or minimised.

> The practical implication is . . . that where professionals are confronted with an alleged female perpetrator who cannot be reframed as masculine, it may be harder for them to sustain the belief that child sexual abuse has occurred. (Hetherton and Beardsall 1998, 1280)

The second point that they raise relates to professional experience of working with females who have sexually abused children. As we have discussed above, generally the number of female offenders that child protection workers come into contact with are very low and consequently caseworkers seem to resort to personal bias and social stereotypes in order to cope with this unusual behaviour. Hetherton and Beardsall's research showed that it was only the female police officers, who had greater experience of working with women who abuse, who recognised that 'femininity and sexual abuse of children can co-occur' (Hetherton and Beardsall 1998, 1280). In general, the other police officers and social workers in their study found this too difficult to align with their expectations. So social and personal stereotyping may be employed when dealing with cases involving female sexual abusers, especially when evidence is ambiguous.

Personal Boundaries

This leads us to a second barrier in relation to professional practice, that which concerns the personal boundaries and bias of individual practitioners. Faller (1993) recognised that, regardless of any amount of training and education, child sexual abuse arouses emotional responses in the professionals who work in the field. Dealing with child sexual abuse is likely to engender one of two responses either 'disbelief or belief accompanied by an intense desire for retribution' (Faller 1993, 1), and this may be accentuated by any past experience of abuse suffered in childhood. Disbelief and denial have a long history, from Freud to recovered memory and beyond. Furthermore, there are some particular gender issues that affect the belief system of professionals as far as female abusers are concerned.

> A female professional may be more disbelieving of accusations against women than a male professional because, as a woman, she cannot imagine doing such a thing. However, when she concludes . . . that a mother has sexually abused her children, she may be especially enraged because of her personal experiences as a mother. (Faller 1993, 2)

Simply being a parent may affect the way workers perceive offenders. On the one hand, they may overempathise with the offender by understanding the intimacy of the parent's role and thus minimise any abusive behaviour. On the other hand, they may feel anger because the offender has violated the trust of being a parent (Faller 1993).

Apart from any emotional response generated by dealing with female sexual abusers, there is considerable pressure put on social workers by the public and the media not only to protect children but to get it right. Any public failures can lead to the vilification of the child protection experts within social services and the health care professions by suggesting inadequate or inappropriate action. Skidmore (1995) has named this a 'reverse moral panic.' Either because professionals have intervened too early or too late, it is the child protection worker who becomes the folk devil rather than the deviant offender. Child protection workers are frequently 'portrayed as zealots looking for child abuse where none exists' (Skidmore 1995, 22; Turton and Haines 2007) or as ineffective, underqualified, and poorly supervised, as in the inquiry following the death of Victoria Climbie (Laming 2003). As a consequence, any reflection on working practice weighs heavily on some child protection workers. The underlying assumption, even that of the professionals themselves, is that they should be able to protect most, if not all, children. While we should acknowledge that universal protection is unachievable, any understanding to this affect has not lightened the burden carried by many professionals, as expressed by one social worker

> She was an 8 year old and the punishment for this child being a pain was mum sent her upstairs when they got home and pulled her dress down and burnt her there (with a cigarette). Now that to me is bizarre, but it wasn't until you asked to speak to me and I was thinking about women . . . that has to have to me now a sexual edge to it. And that wasn't even thought of then . . . when you're speaking it out loud you know you think . . . oh God, didn't I ask this, and why didn't we do that and why didn't we think about things in a different way? (social worker)

Another example of professional anxiety occurs around the assessment of risk. Probation officers expressed concerns about the uncertain ways of determining how risky offenders are to the public and particularly to children. In reality, there is little to be done because having served the sentence, attended probation sessions, and been registered as a sex offender, the paedophile can in effect disappear into the community. In any case, those involved with the probation service are likely to represent just the tip of the iceberg because the difficulties in obtaining evidence suggest that only a few perpetrators go through the criminal justice system.[3]

The combination of emotions and stress creates a very high burnout rate for child protection workers, and staff may attempt to deal with these pressures in different ways. They might become addicted to the work. 'It's like a kick . . . a high that once achieved needs to be repeated' (Julia, social worker and therapist), which Julia likened to the abuser's behaviour because it is impossible to let go without a very conscious, determined effort. Alternatively, some staff develop symptoms of acute stress (Turton and Haines 2007).

Apart from the problems of dealing with personal emotions and public pressure, any under-resourcing within agencies can create more difficulties for professionals in coping with child-protection cases, especially concerning the division of labour between agencies (Morrison 1997). Faller suggests that the 'best preventative measure and remedy for burnout is collaborative work' (1993, 6). However, this is rather complicated given that professional organisations may be understaffed and may fail to provide adequate forums for the emotional difficulties of their workers, identifying not coping as a sign of weakness (Morrison 1997). Where the offender is female, there may be no discursive space anyway for workers in organisations not geared to accept female sexual abusers. Yet it is very important for the workers to express and discuss their fears and discomforts 'if they are to become consistently good at handling difference' (Ferguson 2004, 210). The lack of opportunities to discuss emotional responses to difficult cases is reflected in the way in which professionals feel safe and confident in working together since 'The absence of forums where feelings and doubts can be safely expressed leads to defensiveness, and resistance to share and reflect on practice' (Morrison 1997, 192).

Therefore, one of the issues that needs more consideration is the way in which professionals cope with such emotive work and how agencies support them. As Duncombe and Marsden 1998 have suggested, it seems likely that too little research has been done 'on how individuals actually feel about the emotional work they do' (cited in Williams 1998, 250).

Political Pressure and Whistle-Blowing

There is a third barrier that can impinge on the child protection work of professionals and this concerns political pressure and whistle-blowing. It is hardly surprising that child professionals and their organisations are concerned about discussing their work publicly. Of course, there are serious issues of confidentiality to be considered, apart from the problems of a bad press and the pressure of the emotional work. But there are further difficulties for those who want to question methods of practice or who want to challenge official or unofficial reports. Nelson calls this silence 'the most potent weapon of abusers, both individually and collectively' (Nelson 2000, 394). By suppressing and silencing professionals who want to challenge inappropriate or institutionalised practices, we further silence and inhibit child victims and we protect offenders. We cannot expect victims to speak out if professionals cannot find the courage to do so. Although the fear of litigation is a very important modern issue for all professional workers, it is questionable whether the fear of being sued should be a reason for remaining silent, particularly in connection with child abuse (Nelson 2000).

But speaking out is not always easy. Some professionals fear loss of livelihood through disciplinary action if they speak out or are challenged by colleagues, families, and professional bodies, in medical practice for instance (Turton and Haines 2007), and others may experience job loss, as Alison Taylor found: 'In 1987 I was dismissed from a senior childcare post with Gwynedd County Council because I refused to ignore persistent and widespread allegations about the abuse of children in care' (Taylor 1998, 41).

Furthermore, successful whistle-blowing has a price that makes it even less tolerable for the agencies involved. The social service departments involved with the Welsh children's homes scandal (Waterhouse 2000) are expected to be required to pay out record amounts to the child victims. It is important, however, for organisations to take responsibility for any shortcomings, since it is the lack of accountability within the professional bureaucracies and to the public that 'facilitates unethical behaviour and inhibits ethical behaviour' (Hunt 1998, 12).

Overall, any implementation of professional closure or uses of organisational boundaries, as described variously by Witz (1992) and Barrett (1996), appear to be less significant when child protection workers are involved with women who sexually abuse children. Professionals seem to fall back on personal bias and social stereotypes when making decisions about the very few female offenders they encounter within their work. This does not necessarily mean that professionals are more likely to collaborate and work together in these circumstances. But it does show that there are more common grounds between professional groups than might be expected.

DEVELOPING A PROFESSIONAL RATIONALE

Notwithstanding the different organisational imperatives that shape the responses of other professionals to female sexual abuse, there are important common assumptions and practical difficulties that are shared by the practitioners. Professionals tend to draw on similar gendered assumptions and ideas about criminality, the mothering role, and women as victims. Recognising the responses of professionals to female sexual abuse illuminates some of the particular difficulties that emerge for those involved with child protection work.

The Assumption of the Male Abuser

Even when female perpetrators are identified, there continues to be assumptions about the meaning of their behaviour, especially if they co-offend with men. For example, Liz works for the probation service and has been involved with just two female perpetrators. She was surprised by the 'antifeminine' behaviour of her client.

> . . . having been arrested . . . she did not understand or see that (the sexual abuse) as a protection issue . . . And I was gobsmacked, because I thought she would say that he made me do it and that she felt frightened and threatened . . . and I can remember I was completely taken aback . . . I said 'You've got two other children, three if you count your granddaughter.' So if he said 'Right it's Paula's turn now. Let's you get Paula into bed and you hold her hand . . . ' She said, 'Well if he thought it was alright for them then I would let him.' (Liz, probation officer)

Liz had assumed that her client had been coerced into the sexual activity by her co-offender and that she would recognise that. But this situation appeared to be a much more complicated display of interpersonal power. That is not to say that male coercion does not occur. Women live in a male-dominated society, and for some, relationships are abusive and violent, as the following case study shows.

> C was a weak and powerless mother under the control of her partner . . . her partner controlled her by physically, mentally and sexually abusing her . . . she was in denial about the abuse of her children . . . she and her partner have had a long term but volatile relationship with frequent breaks . . . but she always goes back to him. While they are apart C is able to break away from the abusive lifestyle and improve the quality of life for the children. (Linda, social worker)

But we do need to be wary of making assumptions about this. It may well be that perhaps some men are coerced by women or that female perpetrators may act as partners with men rather than as coerced females. However, as suggested by Liz above and in the quote that follows, it is difficult for professionals to move beyond the stereotypical view and envisage the role of women in such situations.

One of the most disturbing ones and they're not infrequent . . . is where mum has helped step-dad or dad groom or physically force the children or young people to have sex with father. And there have been numbers of those. But it's always pretty obvious . . . there was always obvious coercion in it. (Detective Chief Inspector [DCI] Smith)

Denov (2004) also highlighted that female sexual offenders 'challenged traditional sexual scripts' and led police officers to realign the behaviour of these women to sit more comfortably with recognised beliefs.

Police officers reconstructed the female sex offender and her offence around two poles of representation; she was recast as either the harmless benign woman incapable of sexual aggression, or the wanton, unruly woman who is set apart from 'real' femininity. (Denov 2004, 78)

The problem is that when women admit the behaviour and deny male involvement, professionals find it difficult to work with them. Liz's client Martha took pornographic photographs of two young girls and encouraged them to take photographs of her genitals, over a period of several months. Her male partner at the time was never identified and neither of the victims made complaints against him. As well as denying the behaviour was abusive, Martha had consistently denied the involvement of anyone else. The probation officer still feels she was male-coerced.

She was in a relationship at the time the offence was committed, with a married man and she has led my colleague to believe and myself that she was male coerced . . . I'm not taking any responsibility away from her but this man coerced her into taking these photographs. I guess he coerced her into taking the photographs of the victim. (Liz, probation officer)

It is hard to avoid the general assumption of male coercion, and there are still some professionals who explain all female perpetrators as male-coerced. For instance, Julia manages a therapeutic unit for abused children and their families. She suggested that men influence women, not necessarily in terms of individual coercion but as a group, and that women have been changed and perhaps coerced by patriarchy into behaving abusively. In this way, women's agency is completely denied.

Power and control are common elements of child abuse explanations, especially where the adult perpetrators have little other control over their own lives. This may seem a simple explanation to a complex problem, but many of the professionals were eager to incorporate this idea into their understanding and explanation of female abusers. Issues of masculinity and patriarchy, alongside concepts of power and control, are considered within the dominant feminist theory; but they seem to impose assumptions of female passivity and victimisation, not a facility that would often be offered to men if the circumstances were reversed. Many men do have particular power that impinges on the way in which women behave and respond to their own environment, but we cannot and should not relieve female offenders of all responsibility for their own actions. To do so is to deny women opportunity for equality and freedom from patriarchy, not just female offenders, but all women.

Female perpetrators who act alone with young children or adolescents are more readily seen as making their own decisions regarding their sexual behaviour, but some feminists (Young 1993) have suggested that even these women are acting as a result of male power. Such rationale has been explained in terms of past childhood victimisation or current adult experience of domestic violence or accommodated within the wider remit of patriarchy. In other words, women who lack personal power within the public domain may readily use and abuse it in the private one. Again, the ownership of responsibility is lost within this extended concept of male power. Furthermore, despite the desire of feminist research to accommodate personal narratives and share and understand individual relationships and experiences, we are in danger of excluding female perpetrators by ignoring, denying, or minimising their behaviour.

The gradual development of feminisms has enabled an understanding of difference to develop. Many feminists saw the need to incorporate these differences into their theoretical approaches by critiquing mainstream feminism and including issues of ethnicity and class (Bryson 1999; hooks 1981). It would be useful to give more recognition to difference in a more positive way if we are to include female sexual abusers because, as Kelly (1988) suggests, 'If women are to use only their own experience, or that of women similar to them, as the basis of their feminist politics and research practice, how are we to understand and take account of differences between women?' (Kelly 1988, 4).

The inclusion of female perpetrators within feminist theory and politics is difficult because we have no defined way to make sense of such dangerous behaviour in women, unlike the situation with male perpetrators. The difficulty of explanation and identification of female sexual abusers remains a problem even for workers who have been involved at the sharp end of child protection. Annie is a survivor of paternal sexual abuse and has been counselling survivors of both male and female perpetrators for several years. She still finds dealing with stories of women who sexually abuse difficult to understand but recognises the need to make such stories public.

I can't tell you why it is worse for the rest of the world. It might be difficult for us here being sexually abused women . . . it is hard to imagine someone so close to me, to my sex, being on the abuser's side, being on the enemies side . . . you can't conceptualise it in a way, you have to get used to the idea . . . the world has to say no until it is so ordinary that you don't have to say no. (Annie, counsellor/therapist)

Here we are in danger of falling into the trap that Cameron (1999) calls the 'false gender neutrality.' Because it is mostly men who sexually abuse children and because we have adopted a particular view of femininity and women as victims, we make assumptions about the gender of perpetrators. The assumption of the male abuser takes a rather different course for some professionals. They take on the role of protecting the public from the knowledge of female abusers for 'their own good' and to prevent any feminist backlash. Julia (social work/therapist) felt that the public are ready to take account of women as sexual abusers but maybe not for the right reasons.

The feminist backlash if you like has located itself ready for anything that women can be demonised for . . . to declare women as sexual abusers allows this faction to take up arms against all women as well as to minimise the actions of men as sexual abusers . . . there are more men than women who sexually and violently abuse . . . there may be more women than we suspect who do sexually abuse . . . but the emphasis of prevention and detection should assume the male offender. (Julia, social worker/therapist)

Julia acknowledged that there was a difficulty in admitting that women sexually abuse too, whilst trying to prevent a feminist backlash—a problem recognised and discussed within some of the feminist literature (Kelly 1996; Renzetti 1999). But she maintained, 'The reason for female offending is to do with male power, this is where the attention and resources should be placed,' intimating that the outcome of any limitations in the discourse were rather irrelevant.

The Masculinised Woman

Some professionals attempted to explain female perpetrators by assuming that they are more malelike than other women. This is a rather positivist view that hints at the revival of the Lombrosian woman who is a genetic throwback, an atavistic type. Such a woman is not considered female enough, not a real woman, which is the opposite of the male perpetrator, who may be considered too masculine.

The following quotes from social workers suggest that this can be the case.

. . . she was quite a masculine woman, quite . . . again I can picture her. She had long hair and was much bigger than them (her two male co-offenders) much . . . physically stronger than them and she ruled the roost. (social worker)

. . . and she was clearly, noticeably different from the rest of them (the family) . . . poor self image . . . quite masculine, not big built, very, very thin . . . wafer thin. She had long hair but with all due respect there was nothing feminine about her . . . always wore trousers . . . very dowdy looking . . . a bit smelly . . . there was nothing feminine about her at all. (social worker)

Thus, professionals sometimes explain women who sexually abuse by such rationale as 'they become sociological males' (Heidensohn 1985, 130) since this may be the only way they can accept such antifeminine behaviour. When faced with the undeniable fact that some women abuse children, it is just easier to interpret them as different. By doing so, this distances the abuser, as them, from us. DCI Smith has been involved in child protection for many years and could only remember one case where a woman was the prime mover.

I can't help (with the research) because I don't know enough occasions where a woman was the abuser on her own . . . but one occasion it was different; it was something totally different. A sixteen/fifteen year old girl lodging with a couple . . . she had some family relationship to the male partner. And I've no doubt the prime mover was the woman. But that's because she was allegedly gay. And I think that was . . . she had a huge thing about sadism, all sorts of stuff . . . that was unusual in itself. (DCI Smith)

There are some similarities between this case and Rosemary West.[4]

Thus, we can see that attempts at understanding female sexual abusers are limited by our social perceptions of female sexuality. Professionals have few working or social guidelines to use to help them come to terms with such sexually violent women. And it is difficult to conceive that women may get sexual satisfaction from their children given our stereotypical conception of mothers. A social worker in Turner's (1995) study highlights how difficult this can be.

I personally find it very bizarre . . . it's hard for me as a woman to see how a woman could get any sexual satisfaction from that. I just can't identify with it in any way . . . I'm more attuned to men having gratification of a woman at a young age, it's just a matter of degree how young . . . but this is slightly off the wall for me . . . it's completely out of my experience. (Turner 1995, 94)

Women as Victims

There are four ways in which professionals tend to identify female sexual abusers as victims.

Lack of Theoretical Perspective

First, failing to provide an adequate theory for female perpetrators allows professionals to consider them alongside all women, as victims. Such a presumption is unhelpful when dealing with offenders; it means that it is difficult to see them as aggressors. Elaine has worked with female offenders and survivors, and she recognised that the problem was complicated because we do not just treat women as victims; we expect women to be victims. 'Women have internal messages which reinforce their feelings of vulnerability and their subsequent behaviour. For women it's OK to be emotional and in some ways they're expected to be victims.' (Elaine, social worker/therapist).

It is easy and comforting to identify women as victims rather than perpetrators. It takes courage, time, and energy to change our perception against popular dogma. Mendel (1995) identified that the dominant feminist discourse about child sexual abuse encourages us to perpetuate a society of victimised women and male aggressors. One such example is quoted here from a family lawyer. It is unlikely he would have responded so sympathetically if the abuser had been male.

> . . . and again I can't condone or in any way defend an adult who treats a child like that. But she didn't have a chance. Her own emotions were so screwed up. She loved her children . . . she worshipped them . . . it destroyed her to loose them. She wasn't doing it because she was predatory like this scout . . . who has just got eighteen years . . . he wasn't that sort of abuser . . . she was a victim turned abuser in the classic sense . . . as with the older boy in the first case. (family lawyer)

Child-protection workers more readily accept some women as victims than others and this may be due to class, ethnicity, or sometimes their mothering abilities. This is not to imply a deliberate or conscious reflection, but the perception of individuals is controlled by past experience, bias, and professional knowledge. It is this so-called moral conscience,[5] discussed by Worrall (1990), that may be dominant when interpreting behaviour. It may be easier to miss those women who sexually abuse children amongst those who are verbally able and appear to be good mothers. The reactions to videotapes shown in a training programme run for probation and social workers highlight some of the judgements that may be made.

> One woman who was a health visitor . . . describes on the tape how she sexually abuses . . . what she does to the child is actually much less than what the other two women have described. But the reaction of the people shown the video is extreme . . . for a long time we couldn't work out what was happening here. Then we came to the conclusion that this woman was very similar to the training

group . . . it is the fact that this woman is so like us and I think the issue being that means we have to look at something, that could be us and . . . that's a really dangerous thing for us to bear. (Jean, clinical psychologist)

The training programme encourages child-protection workers to accept that women can and do sexually abuse children. But there are difficulties in challenging the traditional stereotypes of femininity and mothering expectations. Here we have an example, which reinforces the idea that while we continue to believe sexual abusers are not like us, we will fail to engage with what is happening.

The Cycle of Abuse

The second way we can make female perpetrators victims is by engaging with the cycle-of-abuse theory. Despite the challenges made by feminists about this theory (Kelly 1988, 1997a), many professionals working in the field have used this as an explanation of child sexual abuse or at least as a major factor to consider. Some cases of sexual abuse do appear to be related to childhood experiences, but research reviews have challenged the validity of this pathway and indicate that the crossover from victim to abuser is far from certain (Rezomovic et al. 1996). As Dick points out,

> There is no clear syndrome of acting out . . . as far as sexual abuse is concerned the likelihood is that the survivor will present with problems of depression, parenting difficulties and self harming activities rather than sexual dysfunction or displacement. (Dick, clinical psychologist)

Taking such a direct focus on childhood trauma moves the emphasis away from social factors and imposes a label on child victims, thus making assumptions about their future behaviour.

There are preventative interventions that move abuse away from the rather institutionalised approach and passive victimhood to an active struggle for survival (Lamb 1999). For instance, Welldon (1988) has found that child victims who have some stable adult or older sibling support in their lives are less likely to be effected by abusive experiences. Children often find ways to resist abusive advances or at least manage them and thereby gain some feeling of agency and control. Failing these, adequate therapeutic interventions 'prevent (the) reoccurrence of abusive child-rearing patterns' (Buchanan 1996, 35). The end result is that not all abused children go on to abuse and not all perpetrators were abused as children.

Another important factor that questions the cycle of abuse was raised by Freund, Watson, and Dickey (1990), who found a considerable number of male perpetrators used false claims of childhood victimisation as rationale for their own behaviour. Their research only involved male abusers; nevertheless, it would seem appropriate to suggest that female abusers may also lodge false claims. Such an allegation rocks the foundations upon which many assumptions have been made, especially regarding female perpetrators. This is particularly the case when we consider how readily the idea of the cycle of abuse fits in with our image of woman as victim, sometimes superseding the position of the abused child. The work of professionals requires an empathetic approach, and it is difficult to turn this emotion on and off at will. Therefore, the empathy for the child may be transferred to the child victim hidden within the adult. It is very comforting to both offender and professional to use an empathetic approach, especially if there has been a disclosure by the abuser of childhood victimisation.

Therapeutic Discourse

A third way in which female perpetrators are seen as victims lies within the use of a therapeutic discourse. Delia (social worker/therapist) suggested that it was easy to move from talking about 'abuser' to using the word *survivor*, especially when working with female offenders.

> Of course, in one sense the client was a survivor of childhood abuse her self. But as yet this client has been unable to recognise and take responsibility for her offence. I think it might be all too easy to assume that her offences are her actions as a victim rather than an abuser. (Delia, social worker/therapist)

At the time of this interview, Delia was working with a woman who had been sexually abused by her mother and then went on to abuse her own daughter. While recognising that, therapeutically, counsellors may need to address past experiences, there is a real danger here of absolving the abuser of responsibility, ignoring the child victim, and minimising the sexual offences. Perceiving the offender as a victim makes her less culpable, which is complicated because working with abusers requires a holistic approach, so any childhood victimisation cannot be readily ignored. The movement of the feminists from the discourse of victims to a discourse of survivors enabled abused children to be re-identified as active agents (Saraga 2001). But it could be all too easy to slip into a discourse for female sexual abusers that denies the perpetrator both agency and culpability and fails to protect the well-being of children.

Adoption of Victim Identity

There is a fourth form of victimisation that may be used by the offender rather than the professionals. It is linked to the child-protection discourse, which in some ways enables perpetrators to identify themselves as victims rather than offenders.

The victimisation of women, and the feminisation of children to some extent, has been reinforced by encouraging disclosures and teaching women and children to 'recognise sexual harassment' (Roiphe 1994, 163). We have given them the permission and ability to recognise themselves as victims. Offenders can and do use this same pathway. Although there is less recorded about female perpetrators, we do know that male sexual offenders claim to have been abused in childhood (Briere and Smiljanich 1993; Groth 1979; Petrovich and Templar 1984), thus gaining victim status.

> Adopting the role of the victim is . . . a classic abuser stance so giving any abuser such reasons or explanations is very dangerous—it may encourage them to think of themselves as not responsible for their behaviour, and thus to continue abusing. (Young 1993, 113)

Of course, it is both undesirable and inappropriate to return to a culture of silence; however, we need to be aware of this process and its possible repercussions. Perhaps as part of the resolution to this situation we could consider ways of social inclusion for perpetrators by addressing some key issues concerning social capital, social isolation, and self-esteem.[6]

MINIMISATION AND DENIAL

> It seems that the recognition of sexual abuse experienced by a child is dependent on an individual's willingness to entertain the possibility that the condition may exist. (Turner 1995, 98)

In the final section of this chapter, we return to an issue raised at the beginning. Despite definitions, policies, the law, and numerous training courses, there remains room for individual interpretation, minimisation, and denial when considering the sexual abuse of children by women.

There is little doubt that professionals sometimes fail to recognise female abusers. In practice, this is less evident than it was, but research has identified that the potential for denial still persists. The form of denial that is used by professionals can be aligned with that of the abuser.[7] While it appears denial is associated with social stereotypes, there is something else going on here, and if we take the notion behind the techniques of neutralisation suggested by Sykes and Matza (1957), then we can correlate some of the methods of denial available for and used by child protection workers. Cohen's (1993, 2001) ideas around neutralisation, denial and the state are of help here. For instance, denial of female sexual abusers starts with the 'it does not happen here' voiced by two police child-protection units, much as Cohen suggested the denial of human rights abuses is voiced by some states. This can be followed by a litany of rationale that suggests what happened looked like something else, for example, in the case of maternal incest and overenthusiastic child care. We have to understand, of course, that the professional child protection workers are not the perpetrators of abuse, unlike Cohen's ideas of the state. Nevertheless, these correlations and tentative ideas are useful when we attached them to those of the victims and the offenders. At the very least, they point to alternative ways of identifying and making sense of responses to female sexual abuse.

Professionals need to find ways of coping with uncertainties. We might expect them to fall back on organisational assumptions, but in cases where there are female perpetrators these assumptions are in short supply. So child protection workers may use their personal experiences and bias and social stereotypes to make sense of these situations, and the resulting rationale can result in denial.

Denial and General Disbelief

Disbelief can vary from total incredulity to offhand indifference, and most falls somewhere in between. One interviewee seemed determined to cover all possibilities without discrediting the idea entirely. Despite relating a case of the 'allegedly gay' female sexual abuser, DCI Smith appeared to discount this incident in a later statement, which revealed a combination of denial, disbelief, and minimisation.

> It just doesn't happen really and when it does it's usually an element of coercion. In fact I can't think of one . . . there were allegations around a single middle aged woman and some young boys . . . but that never really came to anything . . . that's probably the only in-cident over 5–6 years . . . it was just a woman on her own with no element of coercion or anything else . . . it just doesn't hap-pen . . . I don't know what research you've got? (DCI Smith)

Interestingly enough, almost exactly the same question was raised in Denov's work when she was asked how her research was going in a rather dismissive way followed by the comment from one police officer: 'Hey, how are those dangerous, violent, scary female rapists who are on our streets sexually assaulting? . . . I'm scared . . . I only wish they would sexually assault me' (Denov 2004, 72).

Such attitudes can have very negative influences on an entire team of child protection officers and in the current climate of working together may also have some bearing on the way in which other professionals practice. Denial and disbelief do not allow a critical discursive space for practitioners to acknowledge female abusers. Furthermore, it encourages professional boundaries to be erected, thus dismantling any collaborative initiatives. Here we can identify some of the processes that

> . . . work to keep professional belief structure intact, belief structures that are against the possibility that women sexually abuse children, will only make it more difficult for female sexual abuse to be recognised, regardless of the actual frequency of the act. (Allen 1990, 119)

Denial by professionals was highlighted by Welldon (1988), who found that

> . . . on countless occasions agencies have shown signs of alarm, sometimes almost panic, when referring male patients to me as sexual abusers. This contrasts strongly with the difficulty my female patients have often had in being taken seriously. (Welldon 1988, 98)

Welldon suggests that offenders are not being missed, but their stories may be disbelieved or ignored or realigned to fit into the comfort zones of the professionals involved. A good example of such a case is Brenda.

> So I've told you about Brenda who got no charges for abusing those two children for a huge length of time . . . but actually got imprisoned for eighteen months for cutting a policeman's glove with a knife while trying to stop her son from being arrested . . . no wonder she didn't think she'd done anything wrong because the police and social services knew about this and she didn't get any problem from it. (Jean, clinical psychologist)

Gendered assumptions leak into other aspects of policy and practice. For instance, the influential Cleveland enquiry (DHSS, 1988) identified the need for more appropriate, multidisciplinary training for those working with potential child sexual abuse victims and offenders. However, the report 'made a fundamental error . . . in subsuming parents in one catch-all category; both the enquiry and the press failed to differentiate between mothers and fathers' (Hudson 1992, 145). Not only does this failure ignore the very different needs and rights of abusing and nonabusing parents; it overlooked the possibility of maternal incest. Such omissions mean that professionals are slow to accept that women can sexually abuse their children and maybe slow to accept the stories children tell. Some professionals recognise the difficulties there are for practice. 'In terms of females I think we are just behind . . . way, way behind . . . we suggest that there is so much more of it and even professionals aren't believing victims' (Mandy, probation officer).

> Professionals and others are open to the ideas and theories suggesting that women have more internal inhibitors than men and so are less

likely to abuse . . . the social image of motherhood and femininity often masks abusive behaviour . . . professionals may collude with these mothers by assuming they are the protectors. (Veronica, probation officer)

Denial and Mothering

The second factor that can lead to denial is a tendency among some professionals to rationalise the behaviour of female abusers as overenthusiastic, inappropriate, or poor mothering. For the female abuser, the social expectations of the mothering role can paradoxically merge the roles of mother and abuser because

> No-one questions the child rearing process and the behaviour between mother and child gives rise to the ideal opportunity at minimum risk . . . babies are particularly vulnerable . . . daily care such as creaming a child's genitalia could be questionable. (Veronica, probation officer)

For many child victims, disclosing their stories and being believed can clearly be a problem, especially for those victimised by women (Elliott 1993). This is an important issue because most of our understanding of child sexual abuse and the exposure of paedophiles comes from the stories of child victims. The implication is that the disclosures of victims enables not just the exposure of individual cases of abuse but an insight into the behaviour of perpetrators. It is important to recognise the pathway between disbelieving the stories of victims and denying the behaviour of female sexual abusers. The effect on a survivor can be devastating.

> Victims of female perpetrators describe very damaging reactions of shock, disbelief and minimisation to disclosure of their abuse, including being told they must be confused about who the abuser was or what really happened to them. (Saradjian 1996, 8)

Delia has been involved with counselling adults who were sexually abused as children by professional carers. She discussed one case of a male carer who was found guilty of abusing children in his charge over many years; he was sentenced to twenty years. Many of the adult survivors involved in the investigation also disclosed abuse by a female matron, who had no medical qualifications but who gave them 'internals and enemas.' There was no formal investigation of this woman. Her behaviour was excused under the guise of child care. Interpreting such behaviour as care can be used as a rationale for the abuser as well as the professionals and, according to Delia, could be a very subtle way of grooming both the child victim and other adults.

There could of course be other reasons why the case of the matron was not pursued: lack of evidence, for one. However, even in what seem to be more obvious examples, especially where mothers are concerned, professionals find it difficult to reinterpret and reframe the behaviour of women with their children. Deena sexually abused her two sons. They were moved into care by the family court under the Children Act 1989. The boys had been displaying very sexualised behaviour with female adults.

> We had a lot of argument about whether that was abusive or whether it was actually something that might have been more natural. But given what appeared to be happening with the older boy there had to be at least a suggestion that she was condoning this as part of her own gratification. Whether that was a sexual need being gratified or whether it was some other instinct, like a maternal one, which was becoming confused with sexual gratification no-one got to the root of. (family lawyer)

Denial and Gender

As proposed, gender issues may also cause professionals to deny or minimise sexually abusive behaviour by women. In particular, cultural notions of masculinity have denigrated the sexual abuse of boys by women (Elliott 1993; Mendel 1995). It may be considered less important and less harmful than any male abuse and can be identified as an opportunity for boys to be initiated into heterosexual activity rather than abuse. Furthermore, getting beyond this myth is only the start of the problem; as a local detective inspector pointed out, these cases are much more difficult to take to criminal court.

> There's the joke thing of that's impossible because if the bloke's not up for it . . . blah . . . blah . . . blah . . . You can't possibly take that to court 'cos there's no evidence. There is that attitude . . . you don't get any sexual abuse case . . . rape penetration you can look for physical evidence . . . you can find collaborative stuff if you're lucky. (DCI Smith)

In some instances, it is not the lack of evidence but the reinterpretation of the behaviour that lowers the significance of the case, as Nelson's research suggests.

> In conversation with me the investigating detective expressed a rather insouciant view of this case stating 'shit, I wish someone that looked like her (the babysitter) had sexually abused me when I was a kid.' A fellow detective . . . remarked 'the kid's mother is overreacting because

someone's popped her kid's cherry. Hell, it's every guy's dream.' This view, equating the sexual abuse of a male child with 'seduction' or 'initiation,' was not unexpectedly, absent from the detective's report and certainly bears no resemblance to the official policy of the department which was, where at all possible, to charge those believed to have committed a sexual offence against a child.

(Nelson 1994, 74)

While we are loathe to accept female sexual abusers and male victimisation, we are a long way from dealing with daughters as victims. As far as the sexual abuse of girls by their mothers is concerned, a discursive space has yet to be identified, although Nelson's (1994) research did suggest that offences against female victims are more likely to invoke a criminal charge. In general, the silence created by this lack of discourse makes stories difficult to tell and difficult to hear, even for those who are willing to listen.

One woman came to me, she was never in a group . . . she told me . . . the first time she had told me her story . . . that it was actually her mother . . . I asked her a second time . . . I couldn't grasp it that she (the mother) was the main abuser . . . I probably reacted like everyone else. (Annie, counsellor/therapist)

For some professionals, female offenders who appear normal, that is, act within social stereotypes of mothering and femininity, may be judged in terms of femininity rather than in terms of their offence. As in the case of Brenda mentioned above, the Crown Prosecution Service considered there was insufficient evidence for criminal proceedings, and, despite knowledge of her abuse, she was not considered a risk to children. This is not an isolated incident. 'She didn't drink . . . didn't smoke . . . had a job working as a cleaner in a school where she was very highly thought of . . . 'cos she was pleasant and friendly and very approachable . . . nice with the children . . . safe with the children' (family lawyer).

Worrall (1990) has pointed out how easily any association with normal female behaviour allows us to minimise the behaviour of female perpetrators: 'Many women who break the law also have the attributions of normality which . . . tacitly collude with attempts to minimise the consequences of their criminality by rehabilitating them within the dominant discourse of femininity' (Worrall 1990, 31).

Denial and Emotional Response

The emotional response to child sexual abuse may be another factor leading to denial, or at least minimisation of the behaviour. Some child abuse cases are very traumatic, and we need to be aware that on these occasions the abuse a child suffers may be just too gross to be believed. For instance, there has been an ongoing academic and professional conflict regarding the existence of ritual abuse over the past few years. On the one hand, La Fountaine (1998) refutes the notion of ritual abuse in her research, and, on the other, Sinason's (1994) edited book, *Treating Survivors of Satanic Abuse,* contains evidence from a number of prominent members of the caring professions who discuss clients who have been victims of such abuse. In practice, the concept of ritual abuse is also a problem. Julia (social worker/therapist) ran a therapeutic unit jointly funded by the local NHS trust and social services. The chairman of the steering committee was a very influential consultant psychiatrist, and regardless of what the therapist identified, Julia was very emphatic that 'if ritual abuse was hinted at, we'd be closed tomorrow.' Professional conflicts such as these create difficulties for child victims and loopholes for abusers. If abusers ritualise abusive behaviour, then disclosures from children may be ignored or minimised as fantasy or at least exaggerated, especially in cases where child victims are very young.

We have established that it is often difficult to believe that women can sexually abuse children. But if the abuse is particularly gross or unpleasant, we are dealing with a far more complex problem. Perhaps we could use an example to illustrate what I mean here. In the case of Victoria Climbie (Laming 2003),[8] who died at the hands of her great-aunt and her aunt's partner, one of the observations reported by medical staff identified the cigarette burns she had all over her body as scabies. Most of us would find it difficult to believe such terrible abuse. One bruise may be easier to identify and accept than a body covered in burns. These types of injuries are not just consistent with physical abuse; they have sexual connotations as well. Certainly, Hobbs and Wynne have found this to be the case.

> The link between sexual abuse and burns continues to be found in work in Leeds. The premeditated and sometimes repetitive way that adults may deliberately burn children made us consider torture as the only accurate description. However, several medical colleagues were unwilling to entertain this possibility and diagnosed unlikely or exotic diseases. (Hobbs and Wynne, 1994 quoted in Nelson 1998, 15)

It is difficult to know what changes can be made to protect children if confrontation with the physical evidence and disclosures from children is insufficient.

Denial and Grooming

Another factor leading to the denial of abuse by professionals is related to 'grooming.' Some professionals suggested that offenders were able to groom both their victim and other adults, including those adults working with the family, in order to normalise their abusive behaviour. They do this in several ways.

The child victim may be coerced into assuming the guilt for the abuse, by being persuaded to take at least a share in the responsibility and by being silenced with threats. Partners may be encouraged to either turn a blind eye or take part in the abuse. Professionals may be influenced by adult abusers to disregard or minimise any disclosures from the child victim or unusual behaviour. In these and other ways, many sexual abusers use skills that may influence the way in which we perceive behaviour. Sexual abuse very rarely reveals any physical evidence and this allows the opportunity for such abuse to be misinterpreted; offenders use this opportunity to their advantage.

For instance, Linda (NSPCC/social worker) suggested 'the collusion of social workers and health visitors with their client mothers is probably very high.'[9] In her work, Linda has recognised that this collusion is increased when the circumstances are more difficult for the caring parent. In family situations such as single mothers, working single parents, poverty, or inadequate housing, professionals may minimise and rationalise abusive behaviour to the detriment of the child and thus collude with abusers by absolving them of responsibility. Furthermore, the adult abuser may 'befriend' the professional and it is this very relationship that can be used to coerce professionals into complicity.

Adam has a background in social work and has been involved in child protection for a considerable number of years. He currently assesses risk in terms of families and individual adults, identifying how dangerous certain situations and abusers are for children. He believes that professionals have difficulties knowing how to cope emotionally with female abusers because of the unease of dealing with women who break the rules of femininity. This is a difficult area to discuss because of the implications for child-protection workers. Nevertheless, we should realise that working so closely with clients may create alliances that disadvantage children.

Denial and Lack of Resources

Finally, I want to suggest that there is a link between professional denial and the lack of resources that can be deployed. There is a resource problem of dealing with a child victim whose abuser is the primary carer. Resources play a large part in any decision making and this is a particular problem of maternal incest.

> . . . (social services) haven't got the resources to do any-
> thing . . . and this is happening over and over again . . . they
> don't want to identify women sexual offenders . . . they don't mind
> identifying male sex offenders because actually what they can say is

right we'll work with the nonabusing mum . . . keep the children
at home . . . keep the man away . . . we won't offer too much so
long as we keep them there. (Jean, clinical psychologist)

Certainly it is difficult to know where to place the child if the home is
unsafe, especially in view of the recent children's-home scandals.[10] 'There's
a lack of foster homes because of the rigorous checks . . . they've closed
down children's homes because they're a nightmare to run . . . they've
got nowhere to put (the children)' (Jean, clinical psychologist).

Essentially, the dilemma for child-protection workers is what to do
with female perpetrators if they do identify them. There are few therapeutic services for children and none to speak of for this group of women,
especially where no criminal charges are likely. Social workers may prefer
to deal with male perpetrators because they feel more at ease working
with the nonabusing mother. The underlying problem is lack of any real
contingency plans for cases where the sexual abuser is the mother. So it is
sometimes considered more beneficial to keep the family together and at
best attempt to work through any problems or at worst minimise them,
sometimes, perhaps, denying their existence. While there is a guiding philosophy within the Children Acts and the Working Together policy docu-
ment, which urges keeping children at home, those working in the field
have difficult decisions to make in all cases of child sexual abuse. The
appearance of maternal sexual abuse creates even more dilemmas since
traditionally mother has been considered the nonabusing parent with the
ability to offer the child victim a place of safety. Concerns have been
expressed about the problems this situation presents for child-protection
workers.

People won't pick up women offenders and it is because they don't
want to do the work . . . recently I went and did some training in
one London borough and they said exactly that . . . When social
workers . . . do pick up something they're worried about they get
dismissed very quickly and they get dismissed because . . . people are not overtly saying we don't want to find that but they are
sort of saying . . . oh well let's not make too much fuss over
it. . . . They're doing alright and this government new initiative
about let's keep families together . . . let's work with families and
feed into this. (Jean, clinical psychologist)

Most of those female perpetrators that do come to the attention of
social services are not prosecuted by the police. However, while in some
instances female offenders may be separated from their own children,
they can easily become hidden within the community, sometimes rearing,
or residing with, different children, with new partners in new districts, as
the case study of Jane reveals.

Jane, along with others, sexually abused her son and daughter. She has always denied her abusive behaviour. She was quoted as saying that 'the child is sick thinking I sexed him.' However, her son Tim's descriptions of his sexual assaults were graphic: 'Mum thumps the hardest . . . the other woman unlocks the door . . . gets on top of me . . . watch hole in the wall . . . sex rudies . . . mummy sucks me . . . uncle sucks me . . . mum sucks John and Mary.' (Mel, social-work manager, cited from client notes)

This case was referred to the family court, where the result was that in all balance of probability sexual abuse had been committed by Jane and others. Care orders for the children were secured. There were no police interviews and consequently no prosecutions and her whereabouts are currently unknown. The social workers thought it likely that she may be living on another estate and offering her babysitting services. Here we have a situation that was believed, investigated, and followed through and yet the female perpetrator remains unpunished and perhaps unrecognised within a vulnerable community.

Beyond Denial

Some professionals suggest that they have moved forward, but, despite being aware of the existence of female sexual abusers, they are still behaving as though they are in denial. Dick works as a clinical psychologist. He has not come across any attitudes of nonacceptance of female sexual abusers. However, he is uncertain as to whether professionals fail to see sexual abuse by women or see it and do not respond to it. In referral reports he receives from other professionals, such as social and mental health workers, the sexualised behaviour of women with their children is often minimised.

Delia (counsellor/therapist) agrees but takes her ideas further by suggesting that not only have professionals gone beyond denying the existence of female perpetrators; they have moved on towards disowning them. She maintains that by placing sexual abuse, and particularly women who sexually abuse, into a specialist category, professionals have allowed this to happen. These issues and problems are disowned and avoided because there is no real solution 'and in a way increased awareness leads to more avoidance' (Delia). It would appear that we remain fixed in our attitudes despite the fact our knowledge has increased. 'Thus recognition of its existence alone may not be enough to change beliefs about its seriousness, which has important implications for those who disclose sexual abuse by a female' (Ford 2006, 22).

But we cannot afford to be complacent. Despite any suggestions to the contrary, there is little comfort in imagining that long-term outcomes for victims of female abusers and maternal incest are irrelevant to survivors (Russell 1986)—given that some research indicates a high percentage of rapists who were sexually abused by their mothers (Groth 1979).

CONCLUSION

In this chapter we have considered some of the problems that professionals have in identifying and working with female sexual abusers. These conditions work towards the professional blindness that misinterprets the behaviour of women, especially mothers, because socially and professionally they are too complicated to deal with and 'too hot to handle.' I have discussed some possible links between our social stereotypes and the rationale professionals use when encountering child abuse perpetrated by women. There are some themes here that echo with those of the victims (see Chapter 4) and offenders (see Chapter 5).

There may be simple ways of overcoming some of the problems encountered by child protection workers. For example, we could rethink the gender issues by using a basic question proposed by Goodwin and DiVasto (1979): If the adult involved was male, would this be sexual abuse? Although in the original this idea was used when considering the sexual behaviour of mothers towards their daughters, I think it could be applied to all female abusers. Turner (1995) found in her study that changing the gender of the storyline often gives a better sense of defining the act.

Perhaps first and foremost, child protection workers need to move beyond traditional thinking about women, femininity, and mothering in order to come to terms with the female abuser. Koonin (1995) has identified

> practitioners working with children or adult survivors sexually abused by women need to resolve their own anxieties about female abusers. The abuser is often viewed as one-dimensional—a demonic monster or a saint—by the victim and they need help to accept the abuser as a multi-dimensional human being, with strengths and weaknesses, who committed a serious offence, and who may be subject to a criminal charge. This is only possible if the worker is able to take this stance. (Koonin 1995, 207)

The difficulties that exist for professionals hinge on four main dilemmas.

Most importantly, child-protection workers need to accept that real women do sexually abuse children, a notion which violently attacks our social stereotypes and makes working with female offenders uncomfortable.

> People will often say to me how do you do this work? And I say to them I can separate the behaviour from the person and that's how I manage it. Because if you can't value the human being and say this is a human being . . . this is the behaviour . . . I think you would find it very difficult to do the work. But I mean women sex offenders are another ball game really. They're much more difficult. (Liz, probation officer)

In order to achieve some success in confronting professional conceptualisations of women, we need to reframe female sexuality and the mothering role.

Second, change necessitates challenging dominant feminist theory regarding child sexual abuse and developing a new approach towards the theoretical understanding of women as perpetrators. This does not mean a total disregard of either what feminists have achieved or their analysis, but it is important to find appropriate ways of moving forward.

Third, we need to find ways to improve prospects for child victims. We can do this by developing a more open discourse and environment to encourage disclosure and by ensuring professional workers dealing with sexual abuse cases not only work together but remain child focussed.

Finally, we need to develop forums within which child-protection workers can openly discuss emotive issues and professional practice surrounding all child sexual abuse, in particular the challenging cases that move us beyond the comfort zone raising fears and anxieties over management and practice.

> We must find ways of listening to these practitioners so that we can help them to be reflexive and to de-construct and re-construct their discourses and the practices in which they are enshrined. This applies not just to their professional and occupational discourses, but also to the commonsensical discourses of gender and criminality, the good, the normal and the bad which underpin them. (Cain 1996, 471)

The combination of these ideas could lead to a new discursive space for thinking about women as sexual abusers of children.

4   The Child Victim

. . . it does happen. It hits so deep because this is your main care-giver from birth for most of us. It's hard to realise some of the abuse from a mother because she can hide it so well in the guise of 'taking care of you and your health.' Because it isn't 'penis in the vagina' it may be discounted. (victim, cited in Rosencrans 1997, 19)

In this chapter we consider some of the experiences and meaning of child sexual abuse for the victims. It is important to include victim perspectives in order to recognise their role within the current discourse. The stories of the child victims can throw light on why and how some women are able to abuse their children without discovery, restraint, or, in many cases, any recrimination. The identification of the particular problems that survivors encounter enables a more effective understanding of the behaviour of women who sexually abuse children.

PUTTING THE CHILD INTO CHILD PROTECTION

We have already discussed some of the tensions around the sociology of childhood. It is beyond the scope of this book to describe and discuss these in any real depth, but in order to understand some of the difficulties faced by children who are abused we need to be aware of what underlying factors formulate our stereotypical concepts of childhood.

It was Aries (1962) who identified the social construction of childhood by suggesting that it emerged in the post-Enlightenment period of the eighteenth century. Aries's thesis has been criticised,[1] but nevertheless it has remained a very popular and convincing account. Perhaps the important point he suggests is that during this period children were created as different and separate from adults. Paradoxically, this situation has, on the one hand, created more opportunities for adults to protect, care, and control children, though not always successfully, as we have discovered from the professionals in Chapter three. On the other hand, the position of children as other, as less worthy citizens, can leave them more vulnerable and exposed to abuse by those expected to protect them.

The special category of childhood encouraged a plethora of developmental theories to surface and the consequent emergence of bodies of professional child experts. Some of the theoretical ideas are embedded within folklore, such as the allegories of the innocent and evil child developed within the early philosophical thought of writers like John Locke and Jean-Jacques Rousseau (Stainton-Rogers 2000) and the development of personality and sexuality in the work of Sigmund Freud. Some developmental theories, for example, the cognitive ideas of Piaget (1950) and the concepts of attachment from Bowlby (Bowlby 1965; Holmes 1993), still influence everyday work with children and families (James et al. 1998). However, all developmental theory has drawbacks, because it imposes a universal linear cycle of progress from infancy to adulthood. The steady continuum of progress identified within these discourses proposes an assumption of normality that undermines the individuality of the child (Morss 1996) and tends to concentrate on what is lacking rather than what has been achieved (Stainton-Rogers 2000).

For instance, Freud's work has been very influential, especially in the recognition of childhood sexuality, development, and the unconscious. His analysis has revealed the opportunities for self-reflexivity and exploration by understanding the unconscious elements of the personality but has done little to add to our real understanding of children and the way that they experience their lives. 'Freudian theory positions the child as no more than a state of unfinished business or becoming. Within this model, childhood is once again dispossessed of intentionality and agency' (James et al. 1998, 21). It is important that children are granted agency, especially in terms of human rights, as this may open up new opportunities for protection as well as personal empowerment for the child.

There are strong links between the concept of child development, the 'social aspects of childhood' (Prout and James 1997, 10), and the way that childhood is given meaning within a culture. More pertinent to this discussion is 'debates about the sexual abuse of children are deeply embedded in discourses of childhood' (Kitzinger 1997, 170). These two strands are inextricably linked. So it is no surprise to find that concerns about children as individuals and understanding how they experience their lives is missing from much of the contemporary discussion surrounding child sexual abuse.

Contemporary society protects children within a discourse of welfarism, and while this has been well meaning, and moderately successful for some, it has presented problems for those who are victims of abuse for several reasons. Primarily, the child protection/welfare approach, despite all its policies and practices, has failed to protect all children (Lansdown 2001), particularly those who are sexually abused. Another aspect of welfarism is the assumption that parents have the best interests of the child at heart. Clearly, this is not always the case, and if we couple this idea with the assumption that adults are the deemed experts on children's needs and know best, we find ourselves in a situation that denies children any competence, agency, or rights (Lansdown 2001). What the contemporary linear approach to child development achieves is to reinforce the 'ideal type' mothering concept that initiates notions of failure in both mother and child if targets are not achieved. One of the major problems of welfarism has been spectacularly displayed in the enquiries relating to the abuse of children in public care, where children were found to have been systematically disbelieved in favour of the adults who were caring for them (Lansdown 2001, 88).

We can adjust the imbalance identified with any developmental approach to childhood to consider children in terms of their experience of being (James et al. 1998). In order to do this, we need to place the child in context and, in particular, within the context of the domestic space. The family is a key area for most children, but it does not always provide a safe haven, and this needs to be scrutinised in more depth if we are to 'uncover the extent to which this refuge for the child has in late modernity also become so problematic' (James et al. 1998, 53).

So there are two important concerns that emerge here. First, we need to highlight the importance of exploring the space in which children gain their knowledge of the world; in this case it is the intimate world of the family. The second concern is to move away from linear and developmental theories of childhood in order to see the child as an individual. That is not to say we can discard the everyday language and concepts that have leaked from these theses into everyday parlance and practice. It is just to suggest that understanding the lived experiences of children may give the opportunity for an alternative, sociological paradigm to develop.

This discussion appears to indicate that a liberationist approach of children's rights is the answer, but there are dangers for some children because there is a fine line between offering freedoms and rights and exposing them to abusive adults. Part of the fear behind granting children too many rights is wrapped up in the need to ensure the social control of children. Thus, we are faced with both the innocent and the uncontrolled child, and these two aspects become combined in the way we manage children's sexuality. Understanding this concept is important in connection with child abuse because it is within this social paradigm that our notions of child protection have been generated. Any real acknowledgement of childhood sexuality threatens our current version of child protection. If we discard notions of youthful innocence and grant children a sexual understanding and awareness, how can we reconstruct adult/child sex and child sexual abuse? So offering children any rights over their own bodies, particularly sexual rights, feels like opening a Pandora's box. Without at least some move towards such rights, however, most children will be kept within a wall of silence. All of the survivors cited in this chapter had problems with whom to tell and how, even on reaching adult-hood. Despite some displays of resistance (particularly as identified by Dennis, Petra, and Celia), the survivors felt disempowered and unable to prevent or stop the abuse. Kitzinger has suggested

> It is precisely the children who are the most vulnerable, eager to please and easily led who obstinately reject any idea that they have 'rights' and refuse to develop a sense of their own power. Such unexpected conviction from the most vulnerable children is understandable if we accept that a sense of powerlessness may in fact reflect their external reality. Children are sometimes hopeless because there is no hope, helpless because there is no help and compliant because there is no alternative. (1997, 181)

It is difficult to know how to adequately challenge these situations. The debate has begun with regard to physical child abuse and children's rights, within the 'no-smacking' campaign (Saraga 2001); but as far as sexual abuse is concerned, there is an eerie silence. In any event, by maintain-ing the parental right to 'reasonable chastisement' we have highlighted the main tension that exists 'between preservation of traditional family forms, and the protection of children' (Saraga 2001, 232).

SILENCE AND DISCLOSURE

Since many of the survivors in this research have spent time pondering the question "Why me?" it is useful to reflect on whom female perpetrators target. There seems little doubt that, as with all crime, the opportunity for low-risk perpetration is a key factor. As suggested in a previous chapter, abusers may choose very young children to ensure secrecy (Faller 1987; Grayston and De Luca 1999).

Six of the survivors[2] interviewed for this chapter were abused by their mothers from a very young age. Alice was one of these six survivors.

> My mother sexually abused me and my sister . . . this went on from babyhood. . . . What I have are hints and clues, pictures in my mind and the evidence of things that terrify me . . . once I was clean with my legs waving in the air my mother was turned on by the open vul-nerability of my baby genitals . . . I think she suddenly found herself in a situation with babies where no-one would know what she was doing and she would explore her sexual feelings. The world expects mothers to clean and wipe babies genitals and bottoms. (Alice)

Women who act alone usually choose children within the household or children whom they care for in some other situation such as babysitting

(Matthews, Mathews, and Speltz 1991; Saradjian 1996). These victims tend to be young children, easily silenced, over whom mothers have some legitimate power and control and who are too young to appear as credible witnesses in court. These factors mean that such young victims are much less likely to disclose; they may even be preverbal. If we also take into account the stereotypical ideas of mothers adopted by some of the professionals mentioned in the last chapter, then we can see how easy it could be to target these victims and get away with it. Clearly, from the point of view of any debate about rights versus protection, the young child remains very needy and very vulnerable to attack and therefore requires protective and nurturing cover. But the essence of the discussion is important because these survivors found it difficult to tell even when they came to recognise their own experiences of the abusive behaviour.

The way in which both male and female paedophiles groom a child victim is subtle and secret, and choosing very young victims is only part of the process. It is often unnoticed by other adults and is accepted by the child, who subsequently may absorb the guilt and responsibility for the sexual behaviour. Ensuring the silence and compliance of the victim is important, and women, especially those in the mothering role, do have an advantage over their male counterparts. Partly this is due to the close contact publicly legitimised between women and children and partly it is to do with the stereotypical expectations of mothers discussed above. The result is that it is more difficult for victims to talk about maternal incest because we find it difficult to believe. Mothers have the means to silence children because society finds the truth too difficult to contemplate and children find the exposure and possible loss of their mother figure hard to bear.

Sometimes survivors are faced with total disbelief: ' . . . rubbish— women don't sexually abuse children. It must have been the children mis-understanding motherly love' (letter quoted in Elliott 1993, 7).

Occasionally even therapists and counsellors have described sexual abuse by mothers as childish fantasy, reminiscent of Freud, and casting the guilt and responsibility back to the child. 'A child recently told that her mother had sexually abused her, along with the child's father. The therapeutic team took the view that she was clearly projecting and fanta-sising. The abuse by the father was never in doubt' (Elliott 1993, 9).

And this rather patronising, if well-meaning, response to a disclosure shows how such information can be minimised and misunderstood: ' . . . but she's your mother dear, of course she wants a cuddle' (Penny).[3] The attempts of Penny to tell may have been more readily accepted and believed if children were accepted as individuals in their own right with at least age and knowledge related competence.

None of the survivors I had contact with voiced concerns about expressing themselves, although this can be another problem, as Jane's story suggests: 'I was incapable of expressing myself clearly because the words would simply not come out. I existed, emotionally, behind a wall of silence' (Jane's story, Elliott 1993).

However, all of the survivors felt silenced in one way or another. What was also evident, and related to not being believed, concerned the problem of finding the right person to tell. May was very close to her grandmother and aunt, and Petra also spent a lot of time with her grandmother. But neither of these women felt able to reveal their abuse to these trusted adults when they were children. May did not want to sully the special world that existed for her when she was with her aunt or grandmother.

> My aunt died two years ago . . . it was only then that I started to grieve for my grandmother . . . it was sort of like a double whammy. I miss them even now . . . they were very important to me as a child . . . I never . . . I don't think . . . ever felt like telling (to either her aunt or grandmother) . . . I just felt I could behave like a child with them and be quite safe and secure in that and quite safe about what would happen when I was with them. (May)

Petra saw her grandmother's house as a safe haven and thought she might loose the loving relationship with her grandmother if she revealed her abuse. 'But you see I never tell her (grandmother) about the abuse. She asked me; she asked me a lot of times . . . but I never tell her . . . I don't know why but I guess it's . . . I was afraid of loosing her' (Petra).

Petra never knew if her grandmother suspected her parents were abusing her. Somehow that did not matter when she was with grandma. She also had a close relationship with one of her female teachers and on several occasions tried to tell her about the abuse. 'I thought, I will tell her . . . but how could I?' (Petra).

The abuse that Petra suffered at the hands of her parents was extreme, and for many years she chose not discuss it. There are two possible reasons for this. Voicing the experience means reliving it and in some ways accepting the reality of what has happened, which is the painful beginning to any healing process. The other reason has to do with protecting others. Petra found it difficult to tell because she was uncertain whether others, like her teacher, for instance, would be ready to hear her story.

It is worth considering some more general thoughts about 'telling sexual stories' (Plummer 1995). As with other disclosures, such as rape (Roiphe 1994), stories of harm in connection with child sexual abuse assume a universalism that renders the victim invisible as an individual. The abuse is not placed in context, and there is no account of difference such as gender, sexuality, ethnicity, or culture. These tales adopt a familial tendency that fits in with social acceptability (Plummer 1995). All sexual abuse becomes reduced to a single narrative that is definable, diagnosable, and treatable.

The dominant construction of harmfulness of child sexual abuse operates on the assumption that it is a universal phenomenon experienced equally by all children in the world and treatable by the same or similar interventions. (O'Dell 2003, 143)

Perhaps more importantly, the narrative of sexual abuse is positioned in the discourse of development, which leaves the abused as other, identified by the past legacy of victimhood (O'Dell 2003). The act of disclosure—telling the story—labels the victim (Lamb 1999). And the label itself removes any residual agency, leaving the victim passive and unable to resist further victimisation. So not only are narratives conceptualised and streamlined for the sake of social acceptability, but interventions by agencies that are intended to protect the child may result in further victimisation of one sort or another. Although some individual children may be coping and developing small pockets of resistance to the abusive behaviour, telling someone else means facing uncomfortable facts. Disclosure may trigger emotional responses including the need to recognise the behaviour as abuse, feeling the need to take on some of the blame and guilt for not saying 'no,' or assuming responsibility for the sexual behaviour and finally naming oneself as 'victim' (Lamb 1999, 123).

Rosencrans has some interesting ideas extending the sociological reasons why victims of maternal incest remain silent. These relate closely to our social notions of mothering.

. . . if abused children reveal the sexual abuse by their mothers too freely, they risk not being seen as the victims but as so strange that even their mothers didn't love them. They risk making others uncomfortable by challenging the stereotypes and social mantra that 'mothers love their children' . . . It's easier, simpler, cheaper and emotionally less taxing for society to blame the daughters. (Rosencrans 1997, 33)

Petra and May were in some way aware of the strangeness of their abusive experiences—that their stories were different from other sexual-abuse narratives.

For those children who do disclose, there are other problems, sometimes created by the very system set up to protect them. Dennis spent several sessions with his social worker discussing the problems he had with his mother during his abusive childhood: '. . . social services report everything . . . the first social worker I had wanted me to talk but everything I said got back to me mum. So I just clammed up and said nothing' (Dennis).

Louise was sent to school one day with a broken nose, following an attack on her by her mother. She was afraid to say anything to anybody in case her mother found out. 'Nothing was ever done by the school other than (the headmaster) having me in his office and me refusing point blank to say anything' (Louise).

These two accounts seemed to suggest that victims of abuse make assumptions about how others perceive their behaviour and reactions. In other words, they assume that other adults will recognise their victimisation and be willing and able to rescue them, even if they say nothing about their abuse. We could relate this to the overriding ethos of welfarism as we presume adults are the experts, who know what is best, and have the welfare of the child at heart. So victims have the right to expect to be rescued.

Being listened to, heard, and believed forms one of the lifelines for these child victims not just in order to stop the abuse but because incest victims who have social and cultural support are less effected by the sexual abuse. So having contact with a supportive, loving adult, like grandma, is important to long-term well-being (Welldon 1988). Occasionally even this important lifeline falters. Like Petra and May, Celia's relationship with her maternal grandmother was important to her. But when Celia's abuse was disclosed, her grandmother rather brushed the problem aside: 'Nobody except my grandmother said anything . . . she said, hope it's all behind you now . . . glad that rubbish is over . . . put it behind you . . . you get on with your life' (Celia).

As suggested above, the age at which sexual abuse starts affects the way in which children are groomed and silenced by the offenders. Alice, Petra, and May were all survivors of maternal sexual abuse. They cannot remember when the abuse started 'but it was always there' (Petra). May has a vague memory of when it stopped. 'I think it stopped from her (mother) when I was about 4 . . . why do I think that? Because of what she did and the abuse of the others started' (May).

All the survivors in this study have memories of the way they were abused. The point is that if children are abused from a very young age, then there is no need to target or groom them. It becomes part of everyday life; it is normal. This is not to say that the victims like the behaviour or consent in any meaningful way to it, but, as Petra said, it was just always there as part of an everyday family pattern. It is often difficult for children who have been abused from infancy to recognise their abuse because it is so wrapped up within their small worlds. They experience abuse as normal, as one professional put it,

> I mean if they were really so young . . . some children are raised as having abuse as every day life aren't they? It's not just behaviour that starts and they recognise as bad; it's something they know has happened all their lives and they wouldn't necessarily . . . so in a sense the grooming . . . it didn't take that long to groom them because they were so young they didn't need grooming. (Mandy, probation officer)

Encouraging children to respond sexually is a grooming process used by perpetrators, and, once primed, such sexual responses may last for some time after the abuse has stopped, thereby creating difficulties with everyday life and relationships. This was illustrated by the case of Tim. He had been sexually abused by his mother, uncle, and others during the first six years of his life. He was taken into care and found to be in a continuously high sexual state. He was sexually aroused '98% of the time' (social-work manager). Tim was unable to deal with relationships except on a sexual level. Clearly, this is an extreme case, but it not unique, as these two case studies illustrate.

> This is a four year old, she is at herself all the time . . . she will not leave herself alone . . . the woman saw that as the child wanting sex. She forgets very conveniently, that right at the beginning she masturbated this child virtually from birth and got this child to masturbate her . . . whenever the child cried she masturbated the child or the child masturbated her. (Jean, clinical psychologist)

> Towards the end of one of these (therapy sessions) the older boy suddenly made sexual advances to the female therapist, grabbed her boobs, tried to fondle her between the legs. (family lawyer)

Some young children have been sexually abused so often and for so long it has become a natural response to adult attention and perhaps the only way in which they can ensure at least some affection.

For the older victims, the grooming process raises different issues and problems. The child has to be cajoled, persuaded, bribed, or threatened by the offender to ensure silence and compliance. Some children are swayed in the first instance because it gives them the attention and love they long for. Both Celia and Dennis suggested that this was one of the elements that encouraged them to participate in sexual relationships with adults outside of the home.

Celia was sexually abused by her music teacher, and the way in which she was groomed was classical in its approach. The grooming process began when she was about eleven years old. '. . . she was a very good teacher and a wonderful music teacher . . . she took me to concerts, sometimes on my own and sometimes with other pupils . . . she gave us lifts home, but always made sure we had time on our own' (Celia).

Celia told her music teacher that she wanted someone to love her. The teacher said, '. . . I can't do that . . . ' but kept hold of Celia's hand during the conversation. Then came a confusing series of events that really clinched the grooming process. One day the teacher would reject Celia and the next she would 'send for me to come to her room' (Celia).

The behaviour of Celia's teacher, to offer something and then to take it away, can create the longing that becomes confused with love and desire. Children quickly learn to reproduce behaviour such as care giving and care seeking, especially if the behaviour is rewarded by favours or even just some attention from an adult. This innocent response can easily be used by adults to groom their victims.

The sexual relationship between Celia and her teacher lasted for some months until her parents found out, when it was stopped. Neither of her parents spoke to Celia about it; it was as though it had not happened. Until recently, Celia felt this love affair was mutual and equal. She did not perceive it as sexual abuse. Celia did not know that women could sexually abuse children. Perhaps this is an indication of how the heterosexual discourse surrounding child sexual abuse inhibits our ability to believe that women can abuse.

Dennis was abused by his mother from an early age, and he was placed in residential care from the age of eleven. When he was thirteen, he developed a sexual relationship with a female neighbour on one of his weekend home visits. Dennis maintained that this was not just a consensual sexual relationship but that he initiated the behaviour: 'It was mutual, it was me that approached her first, but I think I instinctively knew it would be, it would be OK' (Dennis).

Like Celia, he longed for someone to love him and was sometimes confused when the relationship did not meet his expectations. 'I could just rely on that love, rather than think of the actual sex. I could survive on the love better. When the love had gone I could go back get some more love. But we didn't have what I wanted . . . we just had sex' (Dennis).

Dennis's assumptions about consent blinded him to the grooming process that had been worked out and controlled by his abuser. Although he suggested that he was in charge, other comments indicated that this relationship was out of his control and that he was disempowered. Yet he continued to take responsibility for both initiating and continuing the contact.

> . . . it was too intimate. The too intimate incidences I could not cope with, the . . . for want of a better word, get on get off, I couldn't cope because it was just get on and get off, yes there was the satisfaction that you get . . . but I kept going back which sort of bewilders me now in a way. (Dennis)

Clearly, Dennis felt that his relationship was two-way and mutually consenting, and this image was encouraged by others, especially those who worked with him in the care home. Dennis made no real effort to keep his affair secret; he used it as a status symbol. So the care staff knew of the sexual relationship but felt, according to Dennis, 'OK about it. They thought it would do me good.' Others, such as his counsellor, have different views.

> The photos of him (Dennis) when he was 13 . . . he looks as if he's about 10 or 11 . . . he's very very small, very underdeveloped . . . and at one stage she (his abuser) says to him, 'oh you're so big and manly' . . . and you think you have to be joking . . . he was tiny. But her

perception to get him in be in that relationship . . . yes it's part of the grooming. (Jean, clinical psychologist)

Dennis was persuaded that he was sexy and desirable and manly. His abuser appealed to his immature masculinity, with the desired response that was reinforced by the staff caring for him. Dennis also enjoyed his sexual relationship not just because he wanted love and attention, but, as he put it, it gave him the opportunity to " . . . piss on his mother . . ." At the time of the interview, Dennis still denied that this experience was sexual abuse, although he recognises that it may have been 'inappropriate under-age sex.'

The Western construction of masculinity creates problems for all male victims of abuse. Masculinity is the antithesis of victimisation. It is particularly difficult for those victims sexually abused by women (Mendel 1995), especially their mothers, 'as boys molested by their mothers often assume responsibility for their own molestation' (Nasjleti 1980, 273). Furthermore, as the case of Dennis indicates, the assumption of responsibility can apply to other sexual encounters with older females. The failure of male survivors to recognise their victimisation and their acceptance of the guilt links with the framework of denial sometimes used by perpetrators.[4] We need to find ways in which we can enable male victims of child sexual abuse to be released from the masculinisation of aggression (Mendel 1995) and allow them to recognise their victimisation.

Another issue that impacts on the disclosure of child sexual abuse by victims concerns the behaviour of other adults in the child's life, those who fail to notice what is going on. Listening to some of the stories that victims tell, it is difficult to understand how this can happen. But sometimes the child victim throws out no signals that would alert others and for whatever reason remains silent.

Most of the survivors in this research, however, thought that their victimisation was recognised by at least one other adult, although this knowledge resulted in little or no action. We have discussed the grooming skill of perpetrators and the effect of this to screen the abusive behaviour. Some perpetrators choose to groom other adults and choose to target vulnerable parents.

> Andrea met Lydia a single mother, and her 10-year-old daughter, Daisy at church. They quickly become good friends and spend time in each other's company. Lydia worked irregular hours as a nurse and trusted Andrea to baby-sit. Andrea took pornographic photographs of Mary. (Police case study)

Other child sexual abusers work closer to home on the nonoffending parent, as Smith's work identified:

> . . . it's important to recognise that not only are children targeted and groomed for sexual abuse by individuals who have a sexual interest in

children, but that partners can be similarly targeted and will be groomed to be less effective as external inhibitors to sexually abusive acts. (Smith 1995, 86)

What seems important here is the comparative ease with which offenders can excuse their behaviour, and this is easier within the mothering role. Care, after all, can become a very subtle form of grooming. Mothers are able to set up opportunities that sometimes appear to be protective rather than abusive.

> . . . one offender suggested that she would set her child up. He wouldn't go to bed when his father told him to. He was at risk from his father's physical abuse, so she took over, setting up the opportunity to be alone for sexual abuse to occur. (Eldridge 1998)

Offenders construct opportunities to abuse by targeting and grooming their child victims and other adults. This process is easier within familial relationships. It is hardly surprising, given these skills and circumstances, that professionals and adults in general often fail to identify abusers and child victims remain silent.

ATTACHMENTS AND NON-ATTACHMENTS

The children's response to maternal sexual abuse may be linked to the psychological ideas about bonding and attachment in a way that does not apply to paternal incest. Psychologists such as Bowlby (1988) and Salter-Ainsworth (1991) have suggested the process of attachment and bonding is an internal psychological reaction to the primary relationship, usually with the mother. I do not want to become embroiled in a nature/nurture debate, but there seem to be two forces in play here that create particular problems for victims of maternal abuse. On the one hand, we have the internal psychological desire for a close intimate relationship with our maternal figure, and, on the other hand, we are socialised into accepting the mythical mothering role that has become our social stereotype. These two forces are closely interlinked, and I suggest they can create a strong detrimental impact on victims who experience mothering that falls outside of the expected social norms. As a consequence, the child who is sexually abused within the home is often placed in an exceptionally helpless situation and needs to regain some sense of self in order to survive. It is this condition that creates what Summit (1983) has termed the *accommodation syndrome*.

> . . . the child cannot safely conceptualise that a parent might be ruthless and self-serving; such a condition is tantamount to

abandonment and annihilation. The only acceptable alternative for the child is to believe that she has provoked the painful encounters and to hope that by learning to be good she can earn love and acceptance. (Summit 1983, 184)

Summit's paper does not refer to any female offenders. However, I suggest that the need to earn love and affection is more urgent in survivors of maternal abuse, which results in strong feelings of guilt and responsibility—a response reflected in the research.

Penny accepted much of the responsibility and guilt for the abuse her mother perpetrated, which was reinforced by emotional blackmail.

> . . . she also passed on huge clouds of guilt to me. I remember her blaming me for what went on at times. I remember her being angry with me, and she was very dangerous when she was angry . . . and I remember her looking at me with disgust and contempt. She could also behave in a very hurt way, which made me feel terrible and made me want to do what she wanted me to do. (Penny)

Penny wanted to please her mother; she did not want to upset her or let her down even if it meant she accepted the abusive behaviour, a finding that is reflected in the experiences of other survivors.

> I used to blame myself for most of what happened, but I'm getting beyond that stage. I've never blamed my mother. Consequently, I have no reason to forgive her. My entire life has been spent hypervigilant of my mother's moods and needs. (Lynne's story, Elliott 1993, 136)

Petra found it difficult to move away from her parents. She went on caring for them and living with them long after the abuse had stopped.

> . . . I grew up with mum and dad and two brothers. And it wasn't a question of time, the sexual abuse started immediately from both mother and father . . . I didn't give my mother up until my father had died. It was some kind of pressure on me for being a woman . . . take care of these two people. They were pretty old when they had me. And when my father died she decided to move on to where my brothers live and I just didn't go with her. Even my brothers wanted me to be the mum and do everything for her because she can't do anything alone. (Petra)

There are three issues here that we can usefully consider in Petra's case. First, the case highlights the need that children have for love and affection from parents and the way in which they accept responsibility for caring for them.

Second, the case shows the difficulty of attempting to break away from the abusive mother. When a mother is so sexually communicative with her child and where the borderline between mothering and sex is so blurred, achieving independence is thwarted (Sgroi and Sargent 1993). Yet in order to gain an understanding of our individual selves, we need to recognise the other 'as a separate person' and be recognised as other (Benjamin 1990, 23).

The third issue here is to do with Petra's apparent difficulty in accepting that the abusive behaviour occurred. Indeed, how can she believe that this happened to her and that the perpetrators were her parents? How will the world view her secret? It is perhaps easier to hide behind the curtains of a happy family.

Elliott (1993) suggests that many survivors of maternal abuse have very strong desires to gain and retain the mother-child bond. ' . . . survivors say that, though they hate their mothers for what they did, they still want to be loved by their mothers and would not confront them . . . as one woman said 'with flowers, let alone with the abuse that she perpetrated on me' (Elliott 1993, 10).

It seems that some victims not only resist confronting their mothers with the abuse but refrain from confronting themselves or disclosing it to others. Dennis, now thirty-seven, has never challenged his mother about her abusive behaviour. He still shies away from being too confrontational.

> No, not challenged, I've asked her and now she does (accept some of what happened) . . . at one time she denied everything then she started her own counselling. What happened was when I started seeing (his counsellor) I became very brave with me Mum. I started asking her questions and that sort of set her quite severely backwards emotionally so she went to see her doctor. (Dennis)

Dennis did not want to hurt or upset his mother by confronting her with the abusive behaviour; he wanted to protect her from that. He still visits on a regular basis and talks about her with affection. Dennis is not alone in the way that he displays his emotion towards his mother.

> There's something about a mother. When you're small, she should be the first person to go to if you're hurt; the first person to cuddle, who gives you love and care. So when she abuses you, it leads to an even greater sense of despair than when your father does it. In my dreams I castrate my father and suffocate him. But I can't attack my mother. I'm torn between love and hate. (survivor, cited in Elliott 1993, 10)

In Chapter two we discussed the ambiguous feelings that mothers may experience, and here the ambiguities appear to be reflected within the experiences of some victims as well.

Louise is another survivor of maternal incest who has never confronted her mother with her childhood abuse. She still has regular contact and goes on weekly shopping trips with her.

> This particular week, it was on a Friday and I phoned her (mother) up and she said . . . I'm glad you phoned she says, I'm not going shopping . . . And I said I didn't want to go shopping anyway. And this was the first time I'd ever said anything back to me mum ever. I was married and got kids and said to her I didn't want to go . . . I says in fact I never want to see you again. I hate the sight of you. I wish you were dead . . . you aren't my mother . . . she said and what's brought this about then? And I can remember saying . . . you know what this is all about and I'm sick of the way you treat me . . . I can remember going upstairs to Alan and waking him up, crying me eyes out, scared that she was going to come in and belt me. (Louise)

For Louise, the consequences of the abuse she suffered as a child at the hands of her mother lives on. And yet she has persisted, as do many other survivors, taking part in the charade of good enough relationships by coping with her memories and attempting intimacy. The reasoning behind this behaviour seems in part to stem from the desire to have the ideal mother even though Louise recognised that there could be no perfect mother-daughter relationship between them. 'I can remember at Christmas crying that I wanted me mum. I cried loads of times wanting me mum, but not the mum got.' (Louise)

Rosencrans summarised this situation very well when she wrote,

> Mothers have enormous power to validate the lovableness and value of children. This child within us as adults seems to believe that, more than any other person, mother can convince the world that we are worthwhile human beings. Mothers can convince us of that . . . abused children want it. (Rosencrans 1997, 33)

It is this validation of self that maternal incest survivors seek in vain. While many of us realise that this assumption is ill conceived, the myth persists: in the media, in our ideas, in policies regarding child rearing, and often within the stereotypical ideals we place on women. Children abused by their mothers have tales that can challenge the maternal instinct.

> My mother said 'I never wanted a daughter . . . it was just the worst day of my life.' The impression I have of my mother is that after I was born she just didn't want to know. And I think it was . . . 2–3 days before she could even hold me . . . I had this dual personality for my mother. A mother who looked after me, who spoke to me roughly, who never played with me. And the mother who when she was abusing me stroked my head. (Penny)

The comments from Dennis were less damning as he continued to ratio-nalise his mother's behaviour: ' . . . she didn't want kids but then I came along. Back then you didn't get rid of them' (Dennis).

The relationships between survivors and their mothers highlight prob-lems with what psychologists (Bowlby 1988; Salter-Ainsworth 1991) would call attachment. But we can explain at least some of this socio-logically by recognising that it is our idealised notion of the mother that generates the need, the craving, and the loss felt by these child victims.

POWER AND CONTROL

It is not just the social stereotypes of mothers and mothering that are at issue. We need to also consider how these abusive mothers use power to control their child victims and how these victims respond. Several of the survivors' stories aptly displayed the abusers' use of power and control.

Penny was sexually abused by her mother. She now recognises that she was silenced and controlled by her mother's power over her: 'My mother kept very close contact with me. I wasn't allowed, neither my sister or myself, to enjoy many things. I think that was the way of course of keep-ing a secret. You know we didn't do anything at all until we were older' (Penny). Penny's mother had complete control over her children. She did not want them to go out or join other children in games and activities. This behaviour gave Penny few opportunities to disclose and helped to keep the abuse secret.

Dennis was abused by his mother and a female neighbour. He returned home one Sunday afternoon later than arranged. His excuses for this were ignored by his mother.

> . . . and I was imprisoned for a week. That imprisonment meant ev-erything taken out of me bedroom, carpets, bed, curtains, everything, toys. The window was actually screwed down me door, had two bolts put on it, two padlocks . . . she gave me a pot to piss in and bread and water and said if I wanted to take drugs and anything like that, then this was what was going to happen . . . me sister contacted a neighbour and told this neighbour to phone the police. The police actually came round, opened the door, looked at me, closed the door and locked it back up again and outside the door said to me Mum she was doing the right thing I was out of control and walked away. (Dennis)

The powerful control that Dennis's mother had over him appeared to be reinforced and justified because it seemed to be condoned by authority. Furthermore, Dennis may not have been recognised as a victim because he failed to fall into the victim category. As Loader suggests, 'young people have long been positioned outside the boundaries of the "ideal" victim' and this is especially so in the case of boys and young men. 'Official and popular discourse about crime tends to view young people as "trouble" ' (Loader 1996, 92/3).

Louise was sexually and physically abused by her mother. And again, her story expresses the urgent need her mother had to gain complete control over Louise.

> That particular night I came in five minutes late . . . I had been with me mates playing monopoly . . . I was supposed to be in at nine o'clock . . . and her uncle wanted to walk me home . . . which meant we had to go the long way round which made me five minutes late. He came to the bottom of the drive with, me . . . Mum was saying 'Yeah, OK, thank you very much; thanks for walking her home' and as soon as the door closed that was it . . . 'How dare you be five minutes late blah blah blah . . . 'that's when she started fighting me again . . . she's never kicked me. We had a long shoe horn and I used to get the shoe horn. She used to duck me, drag me upstairs by me hair. Drag me about with me hair a lot. Slap me in the face . . . fill the wash basin up with cold water and keep ducking me in there. I would take a breath up and then she would belt me again. She actually broke me nose and sent me to school the next day. (Louise)

The abuse Louise suffered was extreme and moved from the verbal and violent physical abuse to sadistic, sexual attacks. Louise used to wet the bed at night despite all attempts by her mother to stop her. Her mother felt annoyed and embarrassed about this 'failure' in Louise and the extra work it created. Louise told me that she felt any so-called failure on her behalf acted as an excuse for verbal, physical, or sexual abuse.

The power and control used by some abusers in cases of child sexual abuse has other side effects that encroach on the victim's developing personality and sense of self. As Giddens (1991) suggested, 'The body is not just a physical entity which we "possess," it is an action-system, a mode of praxis, and its practical immersion in the interactions of day-to-day life is an essential part of sustaining of a coherent sense of identity' (1991, 99). In the case of the child victim, the interaction that takes place between the outside world and the body creates that self-identity.[5] Hence, many male victims have problems with their sense of masculinity (Mendel 1995). Penny described the more subtle aspects of her mother's abuse, which grossly undermined her self-confidence. Her mother was constantly critical of her behaviour and appearance. Consequently, today Penny has great difficulty in coming to terms with her own body.

> . . . and as I grew older and matured, grew a woman's body we had more rows than a normal teenager. Like she always said I had a big

fat stomach and she wouldn't let me wear trousers and she wouldn't let me wear a straight skirt she said it showed my fat bottom. I'd got to wear something that would show my breasts. And then as I got older and got married and got a decent fitting bra she would sort of criticise me. She was always . . . extremely critical of my appearance. (Penny)

Penny feels now that she never lived up to her mother's expectations, but has always remained uncertain as to what her mother really wanted and expected from her.

Other studies have also suggested that female offenders use abuse to control their children (Rosencrans 1997; Elliott 1993), especially at times when the children show independence, as perhaps in the preceding cases of Dennis and Louise.

The problems the women seemed to find the greatest source of difficulty were attempts on behalf of the child for separation and independence . . . (they used) sexual acts with the child as a way of regaining power and control. (Saradjian 1996, 120)

It may be easier for victims and child protection workers to rationalise maternal incest as behaviour that is controlling and violent but nonsexual. However, this fails to accommodate those mothers who also abuse children to gain sexual relief or pleasure from abusing their children. Penny was very young when her mother started to sexually abuse her. She did not know what was happening and did not understand the change in her mother's voice and demeanour.

What she started by doing was pulling me onto her lap and gently stroking . . . she had a far away look on her face. She never spoke to me and she never really looked at me. Whilst she was doing it her eyes never met mine. And then I'd wet myself . . . she'd say oh dear and clean me up. (Penny)

Apart from her own abuse, Petra's one abiding memory of her mother seeking sexual gratification comes from arriving home unexpectedly when she was very young.

I wasn't supposed to be in the house at 2 o'clock in the afternoon . . . I wasn't supposed to be there. I knew that. I knew I did something illegal. I stood watching her what she did to my brother . . . I saw my mother abusing my brother on top of the table in the sitting room . . . you know she had taken his clothes off and put him on the table. She was sucking him and doing things to him and I . . . I remember being angry 'cos she didn't even hurt him. (Petra)

It is difficult to measure the sexual arousal of women, but these two mothers appeared to use their children to achieve sexual satisfaction by abusing them.

Clearly, the behaviour of the mothers of these victims was extreme, but the survivors in this research, and other work (Sgroi and Sargent 1993), report that the fear they have of maternal control and abuse lingers into adulthood.

CONSEQUENCES AND RESPONSES TO ABUSE

For all incest victims, especially those who suffer maternal incest, the most threatening aspect of the abuse is to loose the primary attachment (Sgroi and Sargent 1993). In fact, some abused children never acquire a primary attachment, and so their ability to form relationships and to empathise with others is, at the very least, severely curtailed and, at worst, grossly distorted (Saradjian 1996).

> What . . . sexual abuse experiences have in common is distortion in the meaning and function of sexual activity, so that for some victims sex becomes a way to satisfy interpersonal needs, while for others sex evokes terror, humiliation, pain or guilt. (Watermann and Meir 1993, 14)

As a result of poor primary attachment and atypical, inappropriate sexual experiences, adult survivors who recognise their vulnerable state may avoid intimate relationships altogether. Petra has had a few brief affairs with men. One of her relationships did last 'a year or so,' but Petra pulled out when it seemed to be getting too serious. She has decided not to have children of her own. 'It's been a tough battle . . . it scares me I don't have kids for the reason of coming from this family. It scares me you know I . . . what sort of person does this make me . . . so uhm . . . I don't like to use my children' (Petra). Petra has found that intimate relationships reproduce memories of her past abusive experiences. She conveyed a deep fear about her ability to control her sexuality and sexual feelings, echoing the concerns discussed about the cycle of abuse.

Interestingly, in other parts of the interview Petra's conversation suggested a sensitive and loving response to her friend's son.

> I have been baby sitting and have taken care of children a lot. I know I wouldn't even dream of being like that. In fact this friend had a boy about the same time that I spoke about my incest. And to me he's . . . been the one showing me what a child is all about. So I guess I spoil him in that kind of way. If he wants to do something . . . it's OK. (Petra)

The fear of perpetuating sexual abuse by survivors of maternal incest has been reflected in other research (Elliott 1993; Rosencrans 1997; Saradjian 1996): ' . . . child-rearing was an option foreclosed early and automatically for some daughters as a result of being abused by their mothers' (Rosencrans 1997, 136). Denov (2004) found that same concern among the participants in her study.

> The fear of abusing their children was so strong that several participants reported spending less time with their children or avoided being alone with them . . . Mark was so afraid of sexually abusing his infant daughter that he would wait in another room while she was in the bath. (Denov 2004, 159)

Not all female child victims avoid relationships or maternity. Some survivors may seek out danger and variety in order to achieve some success in terms of sexual gratification. Penny married at twenty-one. Her relationship with her husband was difficult, as he was a very controlling man who often sided with Penny's mother against her. He was emotionally and physically abusive. He wanted Penny to stay at home and 'be at his beck and call' even when he was out. Penny finished the relationship after her three children had left home, and she then began to seek out other partners. She talked about a recent affair.

> He could trigger the warped need syndrome in me . . . that I needed to be dominated. I needed him to assert himself over me. That's what he played on. He suggested quite bizarre behaviour. He raped me. He said I'll blindfold you . . . I'll gag you then I'll rape you. Or he'd say he wanted to do something that would disgust me . . . there was a sort of exhibitionist about him. But he also played a reverse psychology game. He traded with me. He got a job as an emergency plumber. He would come round regularly but sometimes refuse to have sex . . . once he said we can have a drive to the Cotswolds. And I said oh yeah. He said I can tie you up and just leave you naked in the back of the van. And this was terribly bizarre, but terribly exciting at the same time. (Penny)

It is interesting that Penny identified that she had a 'warped need syndrome' that could be triggered and leave her vulnerable. If, as Watermann and Meir (1993) suggest, children who are sexually abused develop distorted meanings to sensual acts, then we could relate Penny's childhood traumas to her intimate adult relationships. For Penny, sexual gratification seems to be entangled with control and abuse and as such are acted out with her as the victim. Maybe this reflects, and in some ways reenacts, her childhood abuse.

Sometimes the controlling element described in Penny's relationship is acted out in reverse so that instead of needing to be controlled, the desire is to be the controller.

One young man was abused in his teens by a much older woman . . .
he cannot have a sexual relationship with a woman if she moves . . . I
mean he can only have a sexual relationship with a woman so long as
she initiates nothing . . . while he's in control that's fine. (Jean, clinical
psychologist)

The controlling desire may display itself more violently, as in the case of Dennis, who physically and sexually abused his own children. He told me this
about his young son Tom.

> At the age of zero I felt I knew what he was thinking. I thought he hated
> me up until he was two I thought . . . 'he hates me.' But he was always
> frightened to death of me. I made him so . . . Tom was a total, totally re-
> enaction of me and Mum, to the point where I even tried to strangle Tom
> . . . I would physically make him tidy them [his toys] up by getting hold
> of him, getting hold of his hand and forcing him to pick each piece up
> and walk him to the toy box to put it in and walk him back. And he'd be
> screaming. He'd be crying and I would continue . . . he would be about
> 2 . . . I'd make him pick each one up, not a handful, each one individu-
> ally and put it in the toy box . . . it was like a torture.

> I had to control. I was a control freak. Still am in a way, got to have some
> control, back then I had to have control of everything. But now I can
> reason. But back then I had to have control of everything, even their [his
> children's] emotions I had total control. (Dennis)

Dennis has found it difficult to come to terms with the abuse he received at
the hands of his mother. He went on to physically abuse his own children
and subsequently received therapy. It was only then that he talked about the
sexually abusive behaviour of his mother. It has had a profound effect on his
life, especially in the way he understands his relationships with both adults
and children.

> The sexual boundaries were just completely and utterly gone. There
> were no sexual boundaries whatsoever, me Mum would get undressed
> in front of us, stark naked . . . she would walk around the house stark
> naked. While we were having breakfast she would actually wash in the
> sink in the kitchen totally naked . . . I became aware of being sexually
> aroused by breasts when I was about 11 years old, 12, when I was with
> me Mum. (Dennis)

It is often the negative messages communicated to the young child as well as
the furtive attempts of abusers to keep 'the secret' that stigmatise (Finkelhor
1986). It took Celia a long time to rebuild her self-esteem following her

abusive childhood. Her father was very emotionally abusive and saw little point in educating a daughter.

> The abiding memory I have is of dad scathing me and contemptuous of things I held dear. I was ashamed for being clever and for being a woman somehow . . . just before I left home I stood up to him . . . he was crushed . . . I always remember being ashamed. (Celia)

Celia's father did not sexually abuse her; she was sexually abused by her female music teacher. But the effect of the emotional abuse perpetrated by her parents contributed to her low self-worth and heightened her vulnerability. Vulnerable children are more likely to be abused and are more easily picked out by perpetrators as victims. Some researchers have even proposed that sexual abuse by women further increases the likelihood and intensity of child victims' vulnerability. Rosencrans (1997) suggested that as many as 60 per cent of the daughters in her study who had been sexually abused by their mothers were exposed to abuse by others.

The story of May illustrates this. She was sexually abused by her mother from infancy until she was about four or five years old. And subsequently she was sexually abused by her friend's brother and then his father.

> The abuse of the others (started) when I was about 5 . . . had I had a better relationship with her then I would have spoken to her what was starting to happen with the others. So . . . if I could have spoken to her, as a 5 year-old when the things that were happening weren't so severe, then other things wouldn't have followed. So eh . . . I 'm really annoyed that didn't happen. (May)

May feels now that it was the lack of ability to confide in her mother about her subsequent abuse, which allowed it to continue. What she does not talk about or maybe does not recognise is that she was likely to have been sexually primed by her mother's behaviour.

Petra's abuse was all consuming. She remembers her father sexually abusing her from a very early age. 'The first abuse I remember from my father I was a few months old and he was using his fingers. But I don't know when my mother's abuse started' (Petra).

Her mother ignored the abusive behaviour of her father as she explained: 'My father abused me in the bed next to my mother . . . as he was lying next to her on the bed all she did was turn her face away. But I don't think my father knew about her abuse part' (Petra).

The sexual, physical and emotional abuse Petra received at the hands of her mother and her father left her feeling very vulnerable. 'She [mother] used to tell me I was a nobody . . . it's all this feeling and all this pain . . . you don't know what to do with all this pain' (Petra).

In her early teens, Petra was raped by her older brother; she must have presented as an easy victim.

All child victims of sexual abuse suffer a sense of betrayal to some degree or other and the closer the relationship the greater the betrayal. For those children who are blamed or disbelieved, the experience of betrayal is further emphasised (Finkelhor 1984). The consequences of such perfidy can have devastating affects for the child victim : ' . . . extreme dependency or impaired ability to trust others, difficulty judging the trustworthiness of others, anger, hostility, grief and depression' (Mendel 1995, 75).

These consequences are displayed in examples from the research.

> But how has it affected me? It has affected me in having relationships. It has affected me in that I don't trust . . . umm . . actually, I would say it's more about women than me . . . I think I have more trust in men than women . . . I still haven't got confidence. I can portray it but I don't . . . it's a mask. All those people see this external thing that Louise can do this, that and the other and suggests this that and the other but inside I'm not. (Louise)

Louise has found it difficult to form friendships, particularly with women. Most of her relationships with men have been sexual, so she has always felt a sense of loss in terms of friendship. Penny was very clear about the effect of her mother's abusive behaviour: ' . . . your capacity to know who to trust, who to love has been warped' (Penny).

As a child, Penny felt abandoned and so consumed by her powerful mother that she feared she would be reabsorbed into the maternal body without anybody noticing or rescuing her. She was encouraged to examine her mother's genital area and digitally masturbate her mother to orgasm. Sometimes Penny had her hand and wrist forced into her mother's vagina.

> . . . and then she said well inside there's a little hole and that's where you were when you were a bit younger and you popped out. And I remember being absolutely terrified because if I had popped out I could pop back in . . . it was difficult because I was frightened of her reaction and there was something in me that said what was going on was wrong but . . . somehow there was just the two of us and the rest of the world was going on without us. I didn't know what was going on . . . I just felt if I got back in no-one would know I was there. (Penny)

Dennis's sense of betrayal has made him feel angry and out of control.

> I'm annoyed because I couldn't express meself . . . I hadn't been allowed to grow up . . . I didn't know what being a child was actually like, that had been snatched away from me when I was six weeks old

. . . It's buggered me life up for something that I wasn't actually in charge of and that annoys me profusely. (Dennis)

Betrayal of trust has a long-term impact on children, especially if the adult involved is a parent (Valios 2001). It is this reaction, combined with the sense of powerlessness, that engulfs sexually abused children and may have a long-lasting and devastating impact on the way they live their lives.

FINDING ESCAPE ROUTES

While we are considering the responses of child victims we need to account for the way in which children can and sometimes do resist abuse. Kitzinger described ways children struggle to cope with abusive experiences.

> Rather than . . . engaging in the unequal struggle of direct physical combat, children employ the strategies of the most oppressed, dispossessed and victimized, joking and gossip, passive resistance and underground rebellion. My own research involving interviews with adult survivors suggests that, although such tactics are rarely recognized by adults, children seek to evade abuse with all the resources they have of cunning, manipulativeness, energy, anger and fear. (Kitzinger 1997, 170)

The resistant response to abusive behaviour by adults can produce an unexpected lift of personal power, which may enabled the victim to confront his or her perpetrator.

Butler (1996) found in his research that children have the capacity, and often do, resist power and abuse through rituals. Child victims can produce an unexpected lift of personal power that may enable the victim to confront his or her abuser. Possible escape routes perhaps need to be considered with some care, as some cases of disassociation have lost credibility in the recent past. What does seem to occur sometimes is that the child can move into a fantasy world during the period of the abuse. For instance, May used this method and in this way absented herself from what was happening to her body.

> I have very vivid memories of the ceiling and shelves above my bed. I think I learned to disassociate from what was happening to me and feel nothing in my body. I think I learned that was the easiest way through it because my mother could certainly pack a wallop if fighting, crying, kicking and such was tried as a way out . . . I was practically smothered at times to keep me quiet . . . what I learned was that it would be over quicker if I let her get on with it . . . I think I tried to escape from her sexual episodes by removing myself as far away

as I could . . . to absent myself from my body while she got sexual satisfaction. (May)

Penny used a different method. She was not aware of fantasising or disassociating in any way. She just knew that, once the abusive behaviour began, the quickest way to stop it was to conform to her mother's wishes.

> She'd just pull down my knickers and when I wet them she'd say I'll get you for that Penny . . . all that extra washing. But she'd change me. She wouldn't smack me or get cross with me as if I'd broken something . . . it was almost a ritual. I learned quite quickly to do it . . . that meant I could get the abuse to stop. (Penny)

Penny and May found physical and psychological pathways to usurp the power of their abusers without having to totally refuse cooperation. This is important, because sometimes confrontation with the abuser can be very violent (Hunter 1993).[6] Once the child victim is old enough, physical methods of avoidance can be used to resist the abuse. Petra avoided some of her mother's abuse by swapping bath times with her brothers. But it was difficult.

> It was more sneaky than that . . . I confused her more by my behaviour . . . taking baths at different times and things . . . she was much more confused . . . I did get dressed at odd times when she didn't expect it . . . I did get a bath when she didn't believe it was me taking a bath. That's how I did it . . . pretend and then kind of switch with my brothers. (Petra)

Louise also locked the door on her mother, but while this produced some small measure of empowerment and relief, there was often a price to pay.

> There wasn't a lock on the bathroom door . . . it was always done in the bathroom . . . the only lock we ever had in any of the rooms was the toilet . . . if me mum come after me I would lock meself in the toilet and she would stand outside and say now you going t'get yours for locking the door on me. (Louise)

By locking the door, Louise sometimes enraged her mother so much that she was even more sadistic in her abusive behaviour. But since this was not always the case, it was worth the risk.

For some, the resistance to abuse took a different turn and became a search for empowerment. This took a variety of forms. Petra had a job not just to escape from the home for periods of time but to avoid having to accept pocket money from her abusive father.

> I had jobs after school. I always did that because I hated to get pocket money from my father. So I was the youngest of the three of us and would rather have a job. When I was ten years old I'd rather have a job than accept any money from him. I remember I don't have to do favours . . . because he doesn't have a grip on me anymore. (Petra)

Interestingly, Petra's tactics gave her little respite from her mother's abuse. Her father was the one who expected favours in return for treats. It appeared that her mother just assumed Petra was hers to use and abuse.

Dennis, who was sexually abused by his female neighbour, used this relationship to annoy and confront his mother, which is how he rationalises his response to the abusive 'affair.'

> . . . in another way I was getting what I wanted which was the love. Also I was pissing up me mother's back and that was another thing. Now I realise that actually I got more of a kick out of that than I did actually out of the relationship in the end . . . because I flaunted it. (Dennis)

The experience gave Dennis back some power and control over at least some of his life.

For Petra, the sexual abuse ended fairly abruptly when she escaped from the household. At fifteen she had the opportunity to come to England to attend a summer school. Her parents had always been keen to appear as a normal, loving, respectable family, so they gave their consent to the trip, which was to be the first of several.

> I remember the first year being in Brighton I sent a lot of letters home about how much I didn't want to go home any more. And believe me it was not a pair of smiling parents waiting for me at the airport. They were angry. But for the first time in my life I thought in my mind, I had a distance; I had stopped the sexual abuse. (Petra)

Although both of her parents attempted to reinstate their abusive behaviour with Petra, she defied them. It was interesting to note that running away from home had never occurred to Petra, and, although it is an option used by other children who are abused (Burton et al. 1995), none of the victims in this research chose this escape route. Perhaps this may be related to the gender and relationship of their perpetrators, since running away would mean recognising maternal rejection.

These examples show how survivors found ways to thwart their abusers and at least in part escape from their power and control. Abused children feel more able to cope with their situation if they have some personal power base from which to operate, whether that is the ability to disassociate, finding strategies to avoid the abuse, or finding ways to confront their abuser.

CONCLUSION

In this chapter we have considered what makes a child vulnerable to incest, especially maternal incest. As with both the professionals and offenders, some of the problems for child victims exist because of the way we have structured mothers, childhood, and the family, and these highlight the limited power abused children have within the domestic sphere. Furthermore, the popular discourse of childhood disengages with the child as an individual and tends to ignore the lived experiences of children. We are only beginning to challenge these stalwarts of society, and we have yet to negotiate reasonable alternatives. But we should, at the very least, consider ways of empowering children, for child protection strategies have failed them (Kitzinger 1988).

While granting children more self-determination seems the logical way forward, moral entrepreneurs would caution such an approach in case it leaves children unprotected. We should be wary of assuming that the divergent needs between children and adults are too broad, lest we play into the hands of some paedophiles (Butler and Williamson 1994). And here lies a dilemma. A liberal approach may expose children to an unfavourable audience with whom they are ill equipped to deal. Protectionism assumes and encourages the innocence and vulnerability of the child, sometimes exposing both to make the child even more powerless.

Within the social context of abuse, some of the child victims do make contingency plans in order to alleviate their abuse, but it is not always easy. The significance of the primary carer is considerable, and understanding separateness and individuality is confused because, as we discuss further in the next chapter, the incestuous mother may see the child as an extension of herself. Children need to be recognised as separate in order to become independent (Benjamin 1990), but some victims of maternal incest remain interlinked with their mothers, encouraged by the social expectations of the maternal role.

We can see from the victim responses that sexual abuse by women is a far cry from the harmless activity suggested by folklore (Allen 1991; Elliott 1993: Mendel 1995). Furthermore, some research suggests there are a significant number of male victims of female abusers within the convicted rapist and male abuser populations (Groth 1979; Lawson 1993; Petrovich and Templar 1984), and current theories of child sexual abuse, including the feminist perspective, are limited in their ability to analyse the situation. This means that we do need to be much more diligent in identifying maternal incest, and female perpetrators in general, to enable the development of new theoretical approaches.

We also need to consider the current models of childhood that are deficient and constructed to supply the needs of adults (Gittens 1993). It would be useful to draw together the ways in which children view their safety alongside the adult concept of child protection (Butler and Williamson 1994).

This is not just an issue for therapists and professionals; it is a research issue as well that requires all aspects of child abuse to be put into social context. And one way to deconstruct child abuse and the female perpetrator is to look more closely at the survivors' stories.

The last words in this chapter must go to the survivors interviewed for this research.

> I was thirty years old when I talked (disclosed abuse) . . . before that you know for the first sixteen years there was sexual abuse, with no hugging going on . . . it was my model. (Petra)

> I was terribly unhappy, I can't remember being happy. (Penny)

> . . . my father wouldn't speak to me for months at a time. I didn't know what I did wrong really. It could be as simple as putting a cup on the table. I think I became a victim without any love or affection with a mother who didn't protect me. (Celia)

We may not have all the answers but we cannot ignore the victims.

5 The Female Offender

Women who sexually abuse children can be of any age, social class, intellectual ability and marital status, and can be involved in any type of employment. They can perpetrate any form of sexual act and can behave seductively or sadistically towards their victims. Some women behave both seductively and sadistically. (Saradjian 1996, 146)

We have analysed some of the difficulties and dilemmas experienced by both child-protection workers and child victims concerning women who sexually abuse. Now I want to consider the female perpetrators themselves.

Any discussion about child sexual abuse creates an emotional response, and if the perpetrator is female the reaction becomes even more emotive. This, as we have seen, can lead to such events being ignored or denied. We need to find some way of conceptualising female offending rather than resorting to denial or pathologising events, since such reactions only serve to perpetuate myths about what it is to be a woman. But perhaps, more importantly, we should develop pathways that allow the female paedophile to tell her story and give her space to voice her experience; otherwise, denial is inevitable. The collation of such narratives could not just enable us to develop a better understanding of individual female offenders but lead us to a more in-depth analysis of all paedophiles. This chapter will look at some of the rationales used by perpetrators and consider ways in which these might be analysed through the vocabulary of motives. In this way, we are moving away from the psychological pathway and traditional criminological approaches and towards a consideration of the wider lived experiences of these women.

In order to contextualise the analysis, there are two aspects that require some further discussion; first, an understanding of sexual stories as narratives, and second, an overview of the justification process through the vocabularies of motive.

SEXUAL STORIES AS NARRATIVES

All story telling is a transactional sequence; in other words, it is a means of exchanging information that is not just one-sided. But any story must be clear and coherent for the teller and the hearer to make contact (Steadman 1986, 132). In order to deconstruct the narrative and discover the reason behind it, we need to understand some of the dramatisation used (Heritage 1984), so that we can move beyond just the story itself and consider the underlying processes.

There are a number of ways we can view the narrative in terms of power, content, and audience. For instance, we can consider whether the narrative is empowering to the teller or not. As far as content is concerned, we can question whether there a discursive space for the narrative and the different listening audiences may alter the way a story is told (Plummer 1995). So in other words, the context in which the story is told, who tells it, and who is listening all play a part in unravelling the meanings. In the case of sexual offenders, what is told is constrained because society is not usually willing to listen.

> . . . this is clearly because nobody will allow it to be told and nobody wishes to hear. It is simply implausible that paedophiles have a story, and inconceivable that they should be allowed to speak it . . . it cannot be heard because of all the 'sexual differences,' this is the one which seemingly creates greatest anger and concern in the wider communities of interpretation. It cannot be received easily. (Plummer 1995, 118)

Developing an acceptable motive and storyline can make it easier to tell sexual stories, but this requires a degree of public acceptance—a collective rationale. Collective story telling requires the community to be 'fattened up, rendered ripe and willing to hear such stories' (Plummer 1995, 121).

So only certain scripts are legitimate, and these exclude the acts of most child sex offenders whose experiences fall outside of the accepted narratives. Therefore, the stories of sexual offenders require a series of techniques or realignments to justify the abusive behaviour in attempting to place it within the realms of 'normality.' Sex offenders carry out 'aligning actions' that not only suggest an awareness of cultural norms but also offer a number of possible pathways to legitimise behaviour (Scully and Marolla 1984, 272).

Apart from the more general problem of storytelling faced by all paedophiles, the way women tell stories is different from men. They tend to situate their stories in context, offering complex detail and depth. This is an important consideration when unravelling the narrative because, if successful, the result is one that sheds light on women's worlds and the way they are experienced.

Women's stories locate women's cultures, women's ways of seeing; they designate meaning, make women's consciousness visible to us. Stories transform our experiences into ways of knowing—about ourselves as women and about ourselves as women looking at the world. (Aptheker 1989, 43)

The explanations offered within the narratives of perpetrators give us a frame of reference for analysis indicating the influence of social structures on the lives of these women. For instance, as we have already seen, some women may move the emphasis of their experiences away from responsibility of offending towards their state of victimisation (Mendel 1995; Saradjian 1996; Young 1993). Becoming a victim creates a more favourable environment with the audience and a more rational motive, one which is not unique to female offenders (Groth 1979; Petrovich and Templar 1984)—although we do have expectations about female victimisation. We are more likely to empathise with offenders who use this approach, finding the excuse for sexual offending more acceptable and thereby colluding with the rationale used.

Female sexual abusers attempt a variety of explanations regarding their behaviour, and I want to consider ways in which we might be able to build a sociological approach from the recognition and understanding of the rationale they develop through their vocabularies of motive.

VOCABULARIES OF MOTIVE—THE JUSTIFYING PROCESS

It is worthwhile at this point to discuss the justifying process in more depth. More than half a century ago in a classic work, Gerth and Mills (1954) suggested that people adopt a verbal justification for behaviour that may be unrelated to the true motive but that is acceptable, or at least is perceived as acceptable, within the social group. Gerth and Mills[1] did not draw a distinction between truth and falsehoods; they were more interested in the fact that all accounts of motivation are drawn from socially acceptable scripts. Perpetrators need to acquire a wide knowledge of recognisable 'grammars' for rationalisations to be adapted to a range of situations in order to gain social acceptance. In this way, we can see how the different vocabularies of motive can be considered as justifications and excuses rather than truths. In the case of female sexual abusers, for example, they can be used to hide any ambivalent 'unmaternal' feelings of resentment or hate from the listener. An examination of this considerable variety of vocabularies of motive can contribute to a sociological analysis of perpetrators on several counts.

First, the chosen motive or cover story is important in itself and may lead to clues of social explanations. It is too simplistic to imagine that understanding motives alone will reveal the 'answer' because sexual crimes involve a 'complex continuum of behaviour' (Scully and Marolla 1984). However, identifying the excuse or justification may enable us to place the behaviour within a social context. For example, Scully and Marolla found research regarding rape has been dominated by the medical model, which has provided a generalised and mythical view of the motivation and rationale of rapists. More importantly, 'the psychiatric perspective has contributed to the vocabulary of motive that rapists use to excuse and justify their behaviour' (Scully and Marolla 1984, 542). The ambiguity here is that while attempting to 'discover' the truth behind the rapist's behaviour, the researchers have provided him with an ideal and acceptable rationale.

McCaghy (1968) suggested that the offender might attempt to excuse and normalise his behaviour in other ways

> . . . by claiming that he had been drinking alcohol prior to the offence . . . (thus) he may be able to admit his behaviour without surrendering his identity as a normal member of society. He can, in effect, substitute a lesser, more acceptable, and temporary deviance for one which is greater and far more damaging to his identity as 'normal.' (McCaghy 1968, 45)

It is worth adding some comment about self-image and identity. As suggested above, it is important for offenders to develop vocabularies of motive in order to remain acceptable and accepted by important others in society. This is especially significant if 'we are motivated by impulses that are disapproved (because) we cannot stand the image of ourselves' (Gerth and Mills 1954, 128). So, if we can manage to make others accept our motivation 'we can understand ourselves and reconstruct our image of self. If we face our motives alone, our sense of unity and identity of self might be threatened' (Gerth and Mills 1954, 128). The motives may be stolen, adopted, or adapted to ensure that offenders gain the acceptability they need to maintain a positive self-image. Understanding the chosen cover story gives clues to the offender's relationship to social structures and how these may restrict the options that are available to construct the storyline.

The second contribution suggested by Gerth and Mills proposes that, as there is a limit to how many and what excuses can be made, these must fall into some recognisable patterns. The repertoire of acceptable social rationale is limited for sexual deviants, especially those who sexually abuse children; female offenders are further restricted by the conventions of femininity. Lyman and Scott (1970) developed some interesting ideas about the rationale of offenders and make clear the distinctions between excuses and justifications. They suggested that 'excuses are socially approved vocabularies for mitigating or relieving responsibility when conduct is questioned . . . justifications are socially approved vocabularies that neutralise an act or its consequences' (Lyman and Scott 1970, 114). Excuses tend to deny any responsibility for the behaviour, whilst justifications admit the act but suggest why it might have been acceptable to behave in that way on that occasion. We will see these excuses and justifications identified later in the analysis.

A final thought on the contribution of this approach to sociological analysis can be identified in Taylor's (1972) work. Although his work related to male offenders, he suggested that the importance of understanding vocabularies of motive are profound because 'once articulated . . . they become the reasons for continuance' (Taylor 1972, 26), and they become internalised mechanisms of social control. So developing a rationale for behaviour that is accepted by the social group minimises the significance of the act and lowers the perpetrators' inhibitions for reoffending. The behaviour can in effect be socially condoned. These motives are the reoffending pathways since 'by winning social acceptance, such motives strengthen our own will to act' (Gerth and Mills 1954, 117).

The above concepts are useful to be considered in conjunction with classical criminological ideas about techniques of neutralisation (Sykes and Matza 1957), which Lyman and Scott (1970) use to discuss their range of justifications for deviant behaviour. Cohen (1993) suggested that state murder and torture are minimised by officials in such a way by a variety of 'excuses' and denial of responsibility. And similar techniques of displacing blame can occur between the perpetrator and the abused child. McLaughlin (2001) suggested what seems to be important in state crime is the ability to rationalise the 'good intention' of the event, even when laws have been grossly violated. There are strong analogies between this official line and the vocabularies of motive voiced by the sexual offender, which are tempered with the reasonable intention of their behaviour. Such offenders do not only indicate their innocence by declaring the 'good intention' (Gerth and Mills 1954) of their actions, but if it is accepted by the audience, they presume permission to continue their abusive behaviour (Taylor 1972).

The vocabularies of motive that are noted here may strike familiar chords with criminologists. However, these declared motives should be considered in context because it is the way in which behaviour is interpreted and experienced by the perpetrator that influences the choice of rationale for particular audiences. Any story only contains what the teller is able to acknowledge, but even then the telling usually creates discomfort for the offender, which is eased through rationalisation. She needs to make her behaviour more acceptable. For example, ' . . . I was drunk . . . ' (Margaret); ' . . . I had to get them clean . . . ' (Janet); ' . . . I wanted to show I loved him . . . ' (Brenda).[2]

Of course, some excuses and justifications are more believable and more acceptable than others. And these form ways for female perpetrators to rationalise their 'out-of-role' behaviour and bring it back into the boundaries of the feminine and the maternal.

VOCABULARIES OF MOTIVE—DENIAL, EXCUSES, AND RATIONALE

Taylor (1972)[3] identified a range of justifications and excuses proposed by offenders regarding their sexually deviant behaviour, some of which have been used as the basis for the following categorisation of the rationale used by female perpetrators.

Denial: 'It Wasn't Sexual Abuse/It Wasn't an Offence'

Of course the most common rationale or excuse for sexually abusing children is total denial. There is no advantage in admitting the truth, and some perpetrators go on denying any wrongdoing until long after their release from custody. Mary Douglas (1992) suggested that denial was used as a forensic strategy to deflect blame away from the offender as deliberate or otherwise, a strategy of defence. Total denial aligns with Cohen's (2001) ideas of denial of the fact of the act; it just did not happen.[4]

Denial of the behaviour is a more practical excuse than any other. There seems little point in admitting the offence since we have socially constructed paedophiles as monsters and social outcasts (O'Carroll 1980; Plummer 1981). Confessions from paedophiles do not elicit sympathy, and the stigma of such crimes remains attached forever. However, while denial may be the initial response, female sexual abusers often alter their rationale slightly by admitting the behaviour, or at least some of it, while still denying it was sexual or abusive. Lyman and Scott (1970) identified this revision of the story as a form of justification: The offender accepts responsibility for the act but either denies it is wrong or at least denies it as wrong under the circumstances.

For instance, Beth took pornographic pictures of her two sons. She denied any abuse and suggested that these pictures were purely artistic. Her husband, the father of the children, supported and agreed with his wife. However, some of the photos were sadomasochistic in nature, showing attempts to cut the boys' penises off with kitchen knives.

Another offender, Andrea, adopted a similar technique of neutralisation when describing her behaviour with Lydia's daughter Daisy. Lydia, a single mother, worked as a nurse and had some difficulty finding appropriate child-minding facilities for her ten-year-old after school and when she did night duty. She was befriended at the local church by Andrea, who quickly became a family friend, confidante for Lydia, and child minder for Daisy.[5] Andrea gradually encouraged Daisy to be photographed. The photographs taken of the girl and taken by the girl of Andrea were grossly indecent.

Andrea ' . . . minimised her behaviour by denying the sexual nature of the acts and one of the distortions was that these [photos] were taken in her own home so that was OK. She suggested that she didn't know she was committing an offence.' (Liz, probation officer)

In Sophie's case, the minimisation of her activities appeared to be based around the affection she had for her children and the way in which she saw herself as a good mother. She encouraged the children to watch sexual acts between her and her boyfriend. The children also had access to pornographic videos.

> Sophie was in denial about the abuse of her children. She felt that the behaviour did not really affect the kids because it was more what the children saw rather then what was 'done' to them or what they took part in. She had an affectionate relationship with the younger children and in a way that fed into her denial because she saw this as being a protective loving mother. (social worker)

Rather than flatly deny the events, sometimes offenders try to discredit the victims and their stories, in other words, deny the victims' version of the events.

> . . . but it still didn't ring true of what they could actually come up with. And what they did say you wouldn't expect a 6 and 7 year old to say . . . some of the things they was saying just wasn't right. You can hear that was part of a set up anyway. They was getting it into their heads to say what to say . . .

> . . . you hear so many stories in the papers what mothers do to their children, beating them up and it makes you feel sick. And then you get accused of it. I mean why would I want to do it in the first place . . . (Janet)

Janet's denial of the children's disclosures seems to be connected to her interpretations of what it is to be a child, an innocent, and what it is to be a woman and mother, nonviolent and nurturing. She attempts by her rationale to realign herself with the norm, and the easiest way is by minimising the events and placing them within the boundaries of nurturing. Janet then used her second statement to reinforce the first by affirming a socially acceptable and expected antipaedophile position.

Using denial as a rationale takes several forms, and as any other evidence unfolds, female sexual abusers may move towards alternative, less dogmatic stories. Here is where the vocabularies of motive begin. In some instances, women may claim innocence by suggesting their behaviour is not sexual or abusive and, as in Janet's case, align it with more socially acceptable perceptions of sexuality and femininity. However, many survivors remember that they recognised the sexual intent of the offences at the time (Elliott 1993; Mendel 1995; Rosencrans 1997).

Pathologising the Behaviour: 'I Was Drunk/I Was Abused as a Child'[6]

The breakdown in mental functioning is a common rationale, because child sexual offenders want to suggest 'a momentary lapse rather than a lifetime of erotic focus' (Howitt 1995, 159) when confronted with indisputable evidence against them. This behaviour has also been described under the heading of an excuse by Lyman and Scott (1970). Unlike the concept of justification, the offender admits the act but denies full responsibility, as her or his state of mind was irrational for some reason.

Margaret masturbated and digitally penetrated her eleven-year-old granddaughter Lisa. From the case notes and discussion with Margaret's probation officer, it seems quite likely that she abused her own two daughters and other grandchildren as well, but the evidence was insufficient for criminal court. She was sentenced to two years' imprisonment. She said she could not remember the incident because she was drunk.

> I'm so shocked . . . it only happened once . . . I was drunk . . . I felt as though I was dreaming . . . it was the day before Mother's Day . . . we'd been to the pub all day . . . I had a boyfriend at the time . . . Lisa wanted to stay the night normally she always slept in the single bed . . . but she wanted to sleep with me, in the double bed. (Margaret)

A second interview with Margaret revealed that further incidents of sexual abuse had occurred between her and her granddaughter.

There is evidence to suggest that substances like alcohol can lower the internal inhibitors that restrict our sexual behaviour (Finkelhor 1984; Saradjian 1996). In any case, it is more understandable, if not more acceptable, if antisocial behaviour occurs when the offender is drunk. Other aspects of social control are important as well. In the case of Margaret, many of her social and sexual boundaries were blurred and therefore behaving sexually with her granddaughter may not have appeared so forbidden to her. And as Taylor (1972) suggests, once any rationale is verbalised and aligned in some way with social norms, the behaviour becomes easier to excuse and may be easier to continue.

It is significant that Margaret was prepared to admit drunken behaviour, which is perhaps rather 'out of role' when in charge of grandchildren, but not the abusive behaviour itself. This reflects the difficulty of admitting sexually abusive behaviour. And although Margaret repeated several times during the interview that she was drunk or she did not know what had happened or it only happened once, she admitted that she understood that as the adult she should not have allowed it to happen and that she needed to take responsibility for the event. It was difficult to tie up these various strands, but it could be suggested that Margaret was trying to cover all eventualities. She felt unable to admit, at least publicly, that she had knowingly abused Lisa. But at the same time, she was well aware that she had to be seen to come to terms with her offence in order to receive favourable parole board reports. This presented quite a dilemma.

Another aspect of pathology to consider is what is sometimes called dissociation (Saradjian 1996). Dissociation occurs as a result of a traumatic event and causes temporary or permanent loss of memory of that event. Sometimes the dissociative state may be provoked by 'events, images or even thoughts associated with that trauma' (Saradjian 1996, 155). Severe dissociation is related to multiple personality disorder, a condition that enables the individual to repress the traumatic events by moving into a separate identity when memory is triggered (Bacon and Richardson 2000; Saradjian 1996). The literature would suggest that this condition is not usually associated with child sexual abusers but is linked to victimisation (Bacon and Richardson 2000; Howitt 1995; Mendel 1995). While this is not a theory taken up by sociology, it nevertheless offers a rationale to perpetrators for justifying abusive behaviour. Even though this rationale is an unconscious form of denial, it enables the female abuser to abdicate responsibility for the sexual offending and may place her in the role of the victim.

One of Delia's (counsellor/therapist) clients illustrates the problems that occur if offenders suffer from dissociative disorder. She has worked for ten years with Mary, who was sexually abused by her mother and then went on to sexually abuse her own daughter. Delia suggests, 'the re-enacting of the abusive behaviour occurred while Mary was not herself. She was in a sort of dissociative condition.'

The sexual abuse that Mary inflicted on her daughter was gross and sometimes sadistic in nature. Here we have the difficult situation where Mary's behaviour was minimised and she was enabled to usurp her daughter's position of victim by becoming a victim herself.

Ideally, offender treatment plans need to include a holistic, therapeutic approach that attempts to deal with past traumas and abusive experiences as well as current offending patterns. It is not unusual for offenders to adopt a victim role as rationale for their behaviour (Mendel 1995; Saradjian 1996). There is no simple answer to this complex state, which requires some careful consideration, if we are to avoid colluding with the abusers. '. . . adopting the role of victim is . . . a classic abusers' stance, so giving any abuser such reasons or explanations is very dangerous, it may encourage them to think of themselves as not responsible for their behaviour and thus to continue to abuse' (Jean, clinical psychologist).

Identifying female abusive behaviour in this way falls in line with the feminisation of victims and the pathologising of antifeminine behaviour, left by the legacy of positivist criminology and 'will mitigate (women's) culpability as offenders' (Hudson 2002, 40). Furthermore, treating women as victims is disempowering; 'It helps to maintain women's internalised patriarchal attitudes' (Young 1993, 113).

Anger is another excuse used for abusive behaviour, which could be classified as a pathological rationale. However, Ray Wyre, who has been working with male sexual abusers for more than ten years, feels uncertain that anger is either an acceptable or appropriate reason for such offending: 'I am always a bit dubious about anger as a motive because an abuser can set up a cycle of behaviour where he knows he will become angry and that gives him some justification for what he does' (cited in Search 1988, 73).

For women, it is less socially acceptable to be angry, especially in public. But behind closed doors and with their children, all this can change. Turner and Turner (1994) suggest that for some women, one way of releasing pent-up frustrations or to gain a sense of relief and power is by sexually abusing. And voicing anger as a motive may offer an identifiable social rationale as well as a personal justification for the perpetrator to continue (Search 1988). If we refer back to the cases of Louise and Dennis (see Chapter 4), we can see how their mothers have excused abusive behaviour as a loss of temper and in that sense blamed the child. In terms of maternal ambivalence, we might consider this response as persecutory anxiety—the mother imagines herself punished and tormented by the child: 'She can feel annihilated, devoured and devastated by a child's apparently wilful determination to humiliate her and frustrate her needs' (Parker 1997, 22). When we limit the discursive space for discussing such ambivalent feelings, then we are in danger of restricting the excuses of some abusive mothers by encouraging them to think of themselves as victims.

Pathologising the behaviour is a common form of rationale used by perpetrators, professionals, and society alike (Allen 1991; Saradjian 1996; Welldon 1988). Child sexual abuse committed by a female perpetrator, especially a mother, is easier to understand if the offender is pronounced either sick, suffering some postvictimisation stress, or under the influence of drugs or alcohol. As far as the perpetrator is concerned, this makes an ideal vocabulary of motive, which, because it is recognisable, aligns with social expectations.

Victim Blaming: 'It Was All Her Fault; She Wanted It'

Victim blaming, also identified in male offenders (Howitt 1995; Taylor 1972) is not an unfamiliar rationale. It implicates the victim and neatly relocates any responsibility. The Victorian legacy of childhood is concealed in this rationale encouraging the mythical notions of the innocent versus the evil or sexually precocious child (Hooper 1992). As we have noted, such dualism creates problems for child protection: ' . . . innocence is a double-edged sword in the fight against sexual abuse because it stigmatises the "knowing" child. The romanticisation of childhood innocence excludes those who do not conform to the ideal' (Kitzinger 1997, 169).

Blaming the child allows the offence to be redefined and minimises the responsibility and behaviour of the adult involved. Furthermore, for some offenders, cognitive distortions provide a framework that allows the behaviour of the child victim to be interpreted as sexual. As Howitt has stated,

> Distorted thoughts are regarded by some as the sine qua non of the paedophile . . . distortions provide offenders with an interpretative framework that permits them to construe the behaviours and motives of their victims as sexual and allows them to justify and excuse to themselves (and others) their offending behaviour. (Howitt 1995, 92)

The justifications made by Margaret illustrate this point. Margaret blamed her granddaughter for the sexual events that occurred between them. According to Margaret, Lisa begged her for sex: ' . . . she wanted it and asked for it . . . she could have left at any time . . . ' Margaret attempted to malign Lisa by suggesting that she was sexually promiscuous—a rationale sometimes adopted by men accused of the sexual assault or rape of women. Margaret suggested that Lisa had sex with boys 'very early' and she had been 'offering blow-jobs for 50p a time to boys at school.' Lisa often absconded from school and sometimes did not come home at night. According to Margaret, Lisa's mother 'doesn't care and can't control her.' Margaret reinforced this rationale with further tales of Lisa's sexual behaviour: ' . . . she was always teasing Tim (Margaret's boyfriend) . . . even at her mum's house . . . she would sit after her bath in her nightie at the top of the stairs with her legs wide open and call him . . . '

It is interesting that Margaret elected to use this approach as part of her reasoning because, as a rationale, it is more likely to be considered in line with social norms of masculinity rather than femininity. Lisa was just eleven years old and some sexual abuse judgements have gone against young girls who are considered sexually precocious,[7] however the existence of a female, rather than a male, abuser is likely to preclude this.

The way that some abusers change the emphasis of stories and what they choose to tell or be silent about creates more opportunities for minimising the abuse and abdicating responsibility. It plays on the myths of children as evil, potentially promiscuous, and liars and it sometimes works.[8]

Cases that involve women who abuse adolescent boys are somewhat different and are often dealt with more sympathetically by the public. Female perpetrators may choose to view young boys as fair targets for sex: ' . . . they take society's view, young adolescent boys want it anyway. They would give anything to have sex with an older woman. It's not abuse' (Jean, clinical psychologist). But a closer consideration indicates that assuming all boys 'want it' is a useful way to justify sexual abuse.

> . . . she talks about this boy as though he was a man. She knew he was far more mature than the others and very different. He was 11, and

> when you see the photo of her with this class . . . he looks a little
> boy . . . but all of the justifications all the way through are very
> clear . . . he was so manly and he was so mature and he was differ-
> ent . . . . he persuaded me to do this . . . it was him who wanted this
> relationship . . . and he is actually saying the same. (Jean, clinical
> psychologist)

It is disturbing when we move female child victims from the category
of innocent to seductive; for young male victims, it creates a considerable problem for their developing masculinity (Mendel 1995). Reports of
recent research in the *Guardian* have shown that boys under sixteen who
have a sexual experience with an older adult female are two to three times
more likely to see a psychiatrist by the age of thirty. And all of this is
maybe reinforced, as suggested by a recent newspaper article, 'If the boy
was under sixteen and the woman older, people sniggered and the boy's
friends envied him' (Bosley, 12 July 2001).

There are some cases where the child victim does appear to 'ask for
it.' The sexual abuse Tim suffered from infancy created an autonomic
sexualised response to adult attention. From this, it is perhaps easy to see
how abusers can blame the victim. Clearly, Tim's is an extreme case but
it is not unique.

> This is a four year old, she is at herself all the time . . . she will not
> leave herself alone . . . her mother saw that as the child wanting sex.
> She forgets very conveniently, that right at the beginning she mastur-
> bated this child virtually from birth and got this child to masturbate
> her. (Jean, clinical psychologist)

In cases like these, we can see how comparatively simple it is for offenders to develop a reasonable rationale that blames the victim for initiating sexual contact. Such justifications for sexually abusive behaviour can
become part of an acceptable excuse, and it has worked for male abusers in the past. This vocabulary of motive picks out our social fantasies
of childhood, femininity, and masculinity. It allows society to perpetuate myths about the evil, sexually promiscuous child who is out of control, and it can reinforce our perception of women as victims and men as
aggressors.

Mothering Skills: 'I had to Get Them Clean. What Sort of Mother Do You Think I Am?'[9]

Some sexual abuse is disguised as mothering behaviour. Our rather
deterministic approach to motherhood creates the opportunity for
offenders to hide behind the childcare banner. We take this further because
we consider mothering a natural instinct, and by doing so we collude

with abusers, minimising suspicious behaviour. Along with all mothers, mothers who abuse are policed by the welfare system, and some are more policed than others. It may be that the overpoliced come to the attention of authority more readily.

Janet knew the policing system very well. She had been involved with both health and social services systems on and off since her first child was born. Both of her children had been in respite care for short periods in the past when she felt she could not cope. Janet knew the 'good enough mother' test and felt she had failed. Part of the rationale she used for her abuse was that she was not 'cut out to be a mother.' Or at least the circumstances in which she was trying to bring children up were not suitable. 'I'm not cut out to be a mother . . . well yes I am but not under those circumstances that I was under. I mean if you find a partner that you really want to be with and you really want children . . . there's no way you can't . . . that wasn't what I had' (Janet).

Janet seemed to recognise that her mothering did not fit into the social norms. The suggestion that she lacks ability, on the one hand, could have been a cry for help; but, on the other hand, it could be used to legitimise her abuse as clumsiness or ineptitude. The latter certainly seems to fit in with her persistent denial of her abusive behaviour. Paradoxically, in spite of Janet's self-proclaimed lack of mothering instinct, she always insisted that she didn't realise her behaviour constituted child abuse; she saw it as childcare: ' . . . you have to get into all the creases . . . I'm talking about the creases in the back of the arms, back of the legs, the neck parts, that sort of creases . . . I used a sponge on them . . . ' (Janet).

In a later interview, Janet did suggest that she now knows what she did was inappropriate, and that maybe her boundaries were inappropriate.[10] However, she did little to explain what she meant by 'inappropriate' or indeed by the concept of boundaries. The terminology appears to reflect a professional discourse rather than recognition of responsibility and culpability.

Janet regularly masturbated her partner's son in the bath. She was also accused of digitally penetrating her own daughter, as well as her partner's, and regularly inserting cream into their vaginas. Of course, there are occasions when small children and infants need treatment as part of their care; however, they are particularly vulnerable, and daily care such as creaming a child's genitals could be questionable. But other sexualised behaviour, still conducted in the name of child care, is less subtle and, like Janet, may begin with acts of masturbation.

> They move on to anal exploration sometimes, under the guise of putting in suppositories, for example, and oral sex. But it's not common for women to get children to masturbate them, that's much more to do with men. With women, it's a compulsion to do to children not to be done to. (Welldon, quoted in Search 1988, 85)

Some female abusers take the notion of 'child care' to the extreme. According to Adam (social work/trainer), one mother who had two daughters subjected them from a very early age to internal physical examinations in order to 'see whether they had been abused or not.' This woman suggested that she also needed to check whether they were developing normally, in comparison with herself. 'It seemed to me that she was justifying her behaviour by rationalising it as childcare.' Sometimes the abuse can be even more violent or sadistic. Following her divorce, Fiona lost custody of her three children because she was in an open lesbian relationship. The two girls were subsequently abused by their stepmother; Cheryl, the youngest, suffered gross physical and sexual abuse on a daily basis. 'Shirley [stepmother] used to bathe her and she'd been rubbing her really hard on the vagina with a sponge' (Fiona). Other behaviour perpetrated on Cheryl, such as being hung from the first floor banisters, was used by Shirley to control her older stepchildren. They were terrified into obeying and maintaining silence, believing that Shirley may kill or seriously maim their little sister if they refused. Despite the sadistic and violent nature of the abuse Cheryl suffered and regular visits to the household by social services, the abuse was not 'discovered' for nearly two years. Incidents such as this are not isolated[11] and perhaps indicate our assumptions about the behaviour of female carers. Ignoring, justifying, or minimising the sexual abuse perpetrated by women may extend beyond the family unit to other carers, as survivors from the recent children's home scandals revealed in Chapter 4.

Several other researchers have suggested that female sexual abuse is disguised as child care (Finkelhor 1984; Groth 1984) and, as suggested by some child-protection workers and victims, there would seem to be evidence for this. While for the actors involved with the abuse there may be no confusion, this is not always the case for outsiders. Female perpetrators who understand the expectations of their roles are able to hide behaviour that has sexual meanings within that which appears ordinary and everyday.

While child sexual abuse commonly occurs in private, some perpetrators may abuse in a more public setting. Such sexualised behaviour is often picked up by the victims but may go unobserved by onlookers:

> My mother and her brothers and father all became sexual around the words 'bottoms' or 'spanking.' My mother indulged in a lot of spanking that didn't really hurt. She rubbed and fondled our buttocks a lot and with a lot of sexual pleasure. There was a special smile she had for this and I saw it again when my sister had children. She did exactly the same to them but everyone thought it was innocent. (May)

The sexual abuse of children by the women who care for them can remain unnoticed because it is unexpected and excused as an extension of normality. We award women the low-risk opportunity to abuse wrapped within the guise of mothering instinct, and, justified by notions of child care, we present the ideal rationale.

Extension of the Self: 'I Felt His Body Was Mine'[12]

The psychoanalytic theory of Freud would suggest that the mother-child bond is the founding relationship that begins the process for the young infant to psychological maturity. It is a delicate balance between maternal overprotection and maternal deprivation (Rutter 1972). Mothers who are incestuous give their children no sense of separateness—no sense of self (Welldon 1988). The mother-child bond can be described as a 'primary love' relationship (Balint, 1965) that can satisfy both the maternal and infant longing through an experience of being one. 'Women get gratification from caring for an infant, analysts generally suggest, because they experience either oneness with their infant or because they experience it as an extension of themselves' (Chodorow 1978, 85).

For many women, it is the mother-child relationship that is the reward, but some use this special situation to abuse their position by creating an atmosphere of possession and ownership, which should be considered, at the very least, unhealthy. 'Some mothers suggest that the bond between them and their child is so strong that no-one can take away that extension of themselves . . . and this continuing sense of ownership must be dangerous' (Eldridge 1998).

So the maternal relationship is a close bond which in time allows for separation, but it is expected to be nonsexual nurturing. Whether caused by a psychological or social misinterpretation or perhaps a sexual desire, some mothers remain so closely linked to their young children that they fail to recognise them as separate.

Alice suffered maternal sexual abuse from childhood and had strong feelings about her relationship with her mother.

> I know that some people who have not been sexually abused by their mothers have deep emotional relationships with them, but I feel that the emotional bond I have with my mother is unnaturally intense. At times I feel that we are almost the same person. Whatever emotion she feels I feel it just as intensely. I wonder if this is because from a very early age it felt like my body was just an extension of hers, and her emotions created the same emotions in me. (Alice)

There seem to be two issues here. On the one hand, some women seem to be unable to differentiate between the maternal role and that of an abuser, and, on the other hand, this is made more complicated because the children involved are less able to individuate and separate from their mothers. Chodorow (1978) notes that daughters in Western cultures have particular difficulties in differentiating from their mothers—a situation that could increase their vulnerability.

> A girl identifies with and is expected to identify with her mother in order to attain her adult feminine identification and learn her adult gender role. At the same time she must be sufficiently differentiated to grow up and experience herself as a separate individual . . . studies suggest that daughters in American society have problems with differentiation from and identification with their mothers. (Chodorow 1978, 177)

Female perpetrators may be influenced in this respect by childhood experiences and lack of suitable role models, which make them less able to differentiate from their children (Saradjian 1996; Welldon 1988). Interestingly, in cases of child sexual abuse, the emotional bond of oneness sometimes carries on even after mother and child are physically separated.

> There were also peculiar things like when she visited them during contact. The younger one (son) in particular would jump up into her arms and wrap his legs around her. But she would then release him, turn him and he would hang down with his head between her legs. And he wouldn't just hang there he would sort of burrow like he was trying to get back into the womb he came from. (family lawyer)

Some abusive mothers voice the way that they feel about their children, like Wendy in the case history cited in Banning, who said, 'I felt his body was mine.' (1989, 565). This sense of possession may provoke a sexual response in female abusers who have the intimate care of young children. The strong identification between mother and infant is socially encouraged through the secure bonding process. However, as suggested above, some mother-child relationships have perhaps moved beyond the sensual to a more overtly sexual stage. The sense of possession may not just be related to the maternal bond but also to a more obvious form of ownership and power: ' . . . vulnerability seemed to be one of the triggers for her sexuality to turn on. Once it was turned on she became another, absent, person who used me as an object' (Alice).

In Alice's case, rather than just an extension of oneness, there seems to be a lack of empathy between the mother and her child. There is some wider evidence to suggest that a lack of empathy acts as a disinhibitor where sexual abuse is concerned (Finkelhor 1984; Saradjian 1996). Clearly, Alice's mother saw her as an extension of herself, nondifferentiated and hers to control, abuse, or love as the whim took her. We must bear in mind, however, that such abusive behaviour could be more closely linked to the child as a sex object rather than any notion of maternal bonding, especially if reinforced by sexual gratification. Welldon (1988) cited such a case in her work.

> She was the only child of a broken marriage, and was brought up by her mother alone from a very early age. Her mother was intrusive to the point of never leaving her by herself. The patient talked of herself as a non-entity, 'just a part of my mother,' unable to make a decision . . . she still remembered vividly how her mother used to get into bed every night, cried a lot and made her promise never to leave her alone. If she promised, mother would 'reward' her by touching her all over, especially around her thighs, which would make her feel very excited. This happened every night. (Welldon 1988, 98)

Janet's need for ownership took a slightly different form. She longed to be needed by her young daughter, and, in order to maintain this, kept her from 'growing up.'

> She wanted to keep her daughter (Tina) a baby . . . she kept her in nappies the whole time . . . she wanted to keep her children dependent on her . . . (Tina) was showing overtly sexual behaviour to other relatives. I think she's been abusing her daughter probably all her life. (Liz, probation officer)

The perception of ownership can become even more overt. Brenda felt her kids were hers and she could do what she wanted: 'I'd had them. Nobody could dispute they were mine . . . you got parents it doesn't mean that they're yours; they could be somebody else's, they're not yours. Whereas your kids when you've had them, you've delivered them, they're yours' (Brenda).

So the idea of a child being an extension of her mother may be accepted as rather a romantic vocabulary of motive because we tend to favour the close maternal relationship. However, it can be used by perpetrators to excuse their sexually abusive behaviour to themselves and others and to hide desires for power and control over their children that result in sexual gratification. For victims, the notion of possession by their mothers can be difficult to break away from and may continue into adulthood, as described in the victim's stories in Chapter 4.

Perhaps the possessive notions expressed by Brenda could be more closely connected to choosing the child as a sex object rather than any confusion with maternal bonding. If such behaviour is reinforced by sexual gratification, then nondifferentiation and possession could be just an excuse. But whatever the actuality of any relationship between mother and child, there is no doubt that the close maternal bond, encouraged by our social stereotypes, offers the exclusive opportunity for the rationalisation of sexual abuse as mother-love.

Desire for Special Experiences: 'It Was Something Beautiful . . . *Something Special* . . .' [13]

It is not just the notion of mother love, but also hopes for romantic fulfilment, that falls within the range of rationale for women who sexually abuse. Langford (1996) has suggested that romantic love could be considered as a patriarchal narrative and is a way of controlling female sexuality. How effective this is in the twenty-first century remains uncertain, but romantic love is still encouraged through literature, magazines, and drama, as well as at the level of political rhetoric, by encouraging marriage and the ideal family units. Although the modern tales may be different, the main goal is familiar: to seek, find, keep, and be supported by the good man. There may be question marks over those women [14] who fail to do this, particularly when children arrive. And some women delight in the mythical image of the knight in shining armour while others prefer the more contemporary emphasis that highlights the right to happiness and brilliant, satisfying sex within or outside of a permanent partnership. Now that we are faced with a weakened family relationship model, maybe maternal incest could be less risky and more satisfying for some women.

So apart from the sexual sensations experienced, some abusive mothers can be looking for the ideal relationship and a hope that 'at last their love will be entirely welcome and put to good use.' (Parker 1997, 22). As Young (1993) suggested, many mothers feel passionate love for their children, and it may indeed be their first experience of unconditional love. This desire for the ideal loving relationship was evident within the stories of abusers, and while there is no reason to doubt these feelings, they were sometimes misplaced. These mothers appeared to expect their children, sometimes before they had even grown out of infancy, to respond like lovers both physically and emotionally.

Brenda very much wanted the perfect loving relationship between herself and one of her young sons, Charles, and in some cases abusers 'may confuse sexual contact with children with genuine affection for them' (Motz 2001, 31). Charles was disabled and Brenda's maternal response did appear to become confused with a more sexually intimate relationship: 'I wanted to show him that I loved him . . . I couldn't put into words how I felt for him' (Brenda).

Brenda sexually abused two of her five children, but it is Charles who falls into the 'ideal lover' category.

> It was like everybody's vision of what they want out of life, you know every little girl wants to grow up and marry the knight in shining armour and live happily ever after . . . when you don't get love and affection you have to fantasise what it's like and its like being really cold, you've been out in the snow then you're coming in and you're defrosting . . . its the warm tingly feelings inside. (Brenda)

Charles' disability meant he needed some special caring as an infant, which would align with Lawson's suggestion that some forms of abuse are a combination of 'the mother's own unconscious need for sexual gratification and the mother's belief that the child needs such special attention' (Lawson 1993, 265).

Janet's situation was slightly different. She had high expectations of her son and was desperate for an unconditional loving relationship, but he never lived up to her desires.

> I expected him to be a lot more than what he was . . . I expected him to cry for his food and wake up at certain times and want cuddles like everyone else told me . . . he wasn't like that . . . I though by perhaps picking him up and cuddling him he'll want to be cuddled all the time . . . he wasn't bothered. (Janet)

In one way or another, both Brenda and Janet 'failed' to achieve what they saw as the ideal mother-child relationship. This failure is partly because they found it difficult to distinguish between maternal and sexual feelings. They were wrapped up in the social presumption that all mothers love their children or can learn to do so (Parker 1997) and that children will respond to their gift of love.

From a sociological perspective, this vocabulary of motive could be seen as a form of resistance to the gender-biased power and control. After all, this may be the only form of control Brenda has had over her own sexuality.[15] Indeed, we could interpret such behaviour as a mechanism of resistance (Foucault 1977), a refusal to accept the narrative constraints on female sexuality. But the changing and unstable nature of contemporary adult relationships must surely play a part in this postmodern world.

> . . . the child is the source of the last remaining, irrevocable, unexchangeable primary relationship. Partners come and go. The child stays. Everything that is desired, but not realizable in the relationship, is directed towards the child . . . the child becomes the final alternative to loneliness that can be built up against the vanishing possibilities of (adult) love. (Beck 1992, 118)

Inner Impulse: The Oversexed and Sex-Mad

Although sexual drive was not identified as a vocabulary of motive in the data, there are two reasons for including this category. First, the notion of the sexual urge to abuse children appeared to be implicit, rather than explicit, in some of the interviews. Second, we do need to consider the very strong motive that gratification and orgasm has for sexual offenders and how this in itself can reinforce any subsequent behaviour. At first glance, this rationale seems more acceptable to use regarding male offenders, since explanations of male abuse could be interpreted in terms of masculinity, as just an extension of the male sexual drive.[16] Male offenders do tend to rationalise their abuse of children in terms of normality (McKinnon 1995), so, for instance, paternal incest becomes an exaggeration of the norm. Acceptance of this reasoning reallocates the blame for sexual abuse away from the father and on to the victim and her mother so that '. . . in the process (of rationalisation) the daughter's presumed sexual agency is pathologised while the natural and uncontrollable response of the father becomes normalised' (McKinnon 1995, 32).

So, though it may be a taboo subject, it would appear that sexual feelings between mothers and their children are not unusual. Breast-feeding, as discussed earlier (see Chapter 2), is one of the more obvious examples used to consider the arousals experienced by women.

> Several mothers told us of their erotic or orgasmic response to breast-feeding . . . one woman welcomed an unexpected bonus of motherhood . . . another woman could not reconcile any erotic response with her concept of the mother role; she never nursed a child again and tried not to think about the experience, let alone confide in anyone for help. (Summit and Kryso 1981)

Mothers may have sensual feelings when breast-feeding their infants that they attribute to the great love and emotion they carry for that child. But could this be a question of attribution rather than different physical sensations?

> You get bodily feelings which can be attributed depending on how you perceive everything in that situation . . . women may see themselves as highly sexual or there is something different in that situation of their child breast feeding or sucking breasts. (Jean, clinical psychologist)

Sexual interpretations of child care do not just apply to breast-feeding. Interpreting the bodily functions such as defecating or the responses of the child such as a smile or a touch, and experiencing it as a sexual feeling, can give an opportunity for paedophiles to rationalise their behaviour. This is partly because sexualising the child in such a way allows the abuser to imagine there is a sexual dynamic between her and that child. And any sexual arousal may be reinforced by masturbation. The pleasure of orgasm is one reinforcing factor that allows taboo behaviour to be repeated and to become addictive, and it does not just apply to the abuser. Once stimulated and sexually aroused, the child can inadvertently encourage the abuse to continue: 'I can't remember feeling sexual when she felt sexual but I think she sometimes created intense pleasure in my body. Not just the normal pleasure of cream or talc, but a more intense pleasure that made me feel helpless and hungry for more of it' (Alice).

There seems little doubt that at least some female abusers have a similar drive for sexual gratification as male perpetrators and that they may have diverse sex object choice or even a preference for children (Mendel 1995; O'Carroll 1980; Rosencrans 1997; Saradjian 1996).

For instance, Margaret had a varied sexual history, including procuring young women and men for herself and husband as well as sexually abusing her granddaughter. According to Margaret's own testimony, she and her husband enjoyed a variety of sexual activities such as wife swapping, threesomes, and lesbian sexual acts. Sometimes Margaret would bring 'young people' back from the pub for sex: 'I would bring men home sometimes with his permission . . . he liked to watch . . . sometimes I brought girls home . . . sometimes he did but usually I did . . . I went with these girls and my husband liked to watch and well . . . then join in' (Margaret).

In the past, Margaret had been accused of sexual acts with underage boys as well as the sexual assault of a seventeen-year-old girl while she was awaiting trial in the bail hostel. Perhaps the most extreme female example observed to date of such behaviour is Rosemary West, but she might not stand alone.

Janet also had wide and varied sexual experiences, and, although she denied sexual abusive behaviour with children, she was convicted of masturbation and penetration of her partner's son. The police also have evidence of her abusive behaviour towards her own children as well as her partner's daughter. The court decided these children were too young to appear as witnesses. So while the rationale of a strong sex drive may not have been used overtly by female offenders, clearly these women can be driven by their desire for certain sex objects.

There is another dimension to consider, namely, that of sexual agency. The concept of mothers as nurturing, caring, and asexual (Banning 1989; Sichtermann 1983) is thrown into confusion if we disclose the behaviour and motives of female perpetrators. 'The existence of maternal incest would intimate that women might have sexual agency, that mothers might not be naturally nurturant, and that fathers might not have power, authority and control over women and children' (McKinnon 1995, 37).

Brenda found that adult relationships failed to provide sexual satisfaction, comfort, and true companionship: 'She had learned throughout her life that she couldn't meet those needs through adult partners . . . so she used children to meet those needs and . . . it becomes reinforcing within itself' (Jean, clinical psychologist).

Could it be possible that for some mothers the only opportunity for sexual agency is maternal incest, and, if so, how does this fit with our notions of mothering?

The opportunity to claim uncontrollable sexual urges as a justification is unavailable for women who sexually abuse children. It is a socially unacceptable narrative for women. While this vocabulary of motive may be socially less than desirable, it is accepted as an extension of masculinity and so forms part of the male perpetrator's narrative. In could be, however, that the traditional way we have constructed our ideas of what it is to be a woman and what it is to be a mother acts in opposition to the sexual drive that some women may possess.

CONCLUSION

There are complications to understanding any child sexual abuse. It is a very covert crime that on discovery provokes a very emotive social response. Clearly, just considering the stories from the victim's point of view is insufficient, and we need to find ways of listening, hearing, and deconstructing the perpetrator's narratives.

This is a difficult process. First, we have to overcome the silence. We have raised questions here about what stories can be told and where and when they are told. We have also questioned how mothers are given permission to behave intimately with their children, offering them the means and opportunity to engage sexually with them. Emphasis on the perfect mother-child bond disguises the ambiguous nature of their relationship and often silences those who feel their mothering does not fit social norms and expectations. This can be a problem for some women, who, as Coward (1997) suggests, can find no other outlet other than to abuse or in some cases murder their children.

Second, throughout this chapter there has been an underlying awareness of the lack discursive space within sociology for considering these female offenders. Here we have a specific group of women whose different lifestyles do not fit easily within most discussions of sexual and violent crime and whose behaviours fall outside of dominant feminist discourse.

Finally, this chapter has viewed the vocabularies of motive voiced by female perpetrators as an attempt to include their stories. We have found women who struggle to align themselves with social norms and so develop a series of motives and rationale to account for their behaviour. True motives may never be revealed; they are either too hidden in the subconscious or too difficult to voice in the current social climate. However, we have to assume that a combination of opportunity, excitement, pleasure, power, and orgasm breaks down the expected barriers of internal controls and ignites the desire to sexually abuse.

It is these vocabularies of motive that reveal social structures and stereotypes that offer perpetrators opportunities to abuse and then deny, excuse, and justify.

6   The Last Word

> Arguably, each time a female sex offender raises her voice she is opening
> the space, within which new knowledge and discourse can be produced
> about women who sexually offend. However . . . each time a female
> sex offender 'speaks,' there are explicit attempts by criminal justice
> and mental health practitioners to mute her voice, her actions and her
> responsibility once again rely upon the 'known truths' about women.
> (Denov 2004, 182)

We have established that, generally speaking, all sexual and most violent
crimes are considered male. Therefore, those women who act out sexually
or behave violently are acting against acceptable feminine behaviour (Koonin 1995). Yet while the criminal statistics are insignificant, this and other
research (Denov 2004; Elliott 1993; Ford 2006; Mendel 1995; Saradjian
1996) show that some women do sexually abuse. So why do even those
working in child protection find it so hard to come to terms with female perpetrators? There is no single answer, but what this book has suggested is the
identification of a series of 'silences' surrounding the narratives of female
sexual abusers that are displayed not just by denials but also by minimisation, excuses,and justification. Such rationales are required, because most
women who sexually abuse need to be aligned with our notions of womanhood. Others, like Rosemary West, at least once they are exposed, may be
disregarded as different and therefore not real women. Thus, the sexual
behaviour is hidden by a variety of explanations in an attempt to find ways
that rationalise female aggression and align it with the social conceptions of
femininity and the maternal (Motz 2001).

Since sexual abuse is such an unacceptable deviant act, any form of denial
offered by the offenders may seem a logical response. However, the denial
of the behaviour by professionals and even the child victims themselves may
appear at first illogical. That is, until we examine the evidence that suggests
that denying or minimising the behaviour of female perpetrators relates to
the lack of discursive space available for such stories to be told as well as the

way in which we conceptualise women and mothers. It is these factors that create boundaries limiting our understanding of women who are sexually aggressive or violent.

LACK OF DISCURSIVE SPACE

For child protection professionals, the problems of identifying female sexual abusers appears to be one of confusion. There has been little practical experience, and there is a paucity of theoretical knowledge to inform this part of their practice; the main debates remain almost exclusively focused on masculinity, aggression, and power. It is the lack of theoretical backdrop to translate into policy, along with limited experience in the field, that encourages workers to fall back onto their personal bias and social stereotypes for decision making. There are specific practical problems to face, because the discovery of maternal incest inverts previous ideology about the family in which the mother has been perceived as the main carer and nonabusive parent. The female sexual abuser creates a disturbing picture when following the guidelines of the Children Acts (1989 and 2004) in an attempt to keep the victims with their families at home. Also, there are significant resource and childcare implications if children require an alternative place of safety.

Another aspect of the discursive space that merits serious consideration, if we are to expect change, is the need for a forum for professionals to discuss any emotional responses to their work. It is difficult to find time to deal with emotional accounts in busy professional lives; nonetheless, granting professionals time and space for such discussion could strengthen staff individually, collectively, and practically through sharing experiences. Furthermore, it would move us away from the current philosophy of some agencies that identify emotional responses to situations as not coping or weakness (Morrison 1997). As far as this book is concerned, it would appear that ignoring emotional responses and uncertainty about sexually aggressive women and maternal incest may encourage professional denial, and there are indications that this may be relevant for other cases of abuse as well (Cooper et al. 2003).

Child victims of female perpetrators find sharing the experiences equally problematic. There is no space for them to tell their stories, and the time never seems quite right. Victims may not reveal their abuse until well into their adult lives, if at all, and victims of maternal incest often have their stories minimised or disbelieved. For male victims, this may be complicated because the sexual experience, especially if accompanied by arousal or orgasm, may be perceived as initiation rather than abuse, as suggested by Dennis in Chapter 4. In cases of maternal incest, male victims may accept the guilt and responsibility for the abusive behaviour within a confusion of developing masculinity. There is yet to be a discursive space for the female victims of maternal incest, and so many of their stories are yet to be heard (Rosencrans 1997). Listening to the narratives offers us an insight into the behaviour of perpetrators and the interaction between the abuser and the child. Perhaps more significantly, it enables us to gain some indication about how the victim rationalises the abuse and the ways in which it is resisted.

Not surprisingly, women who sexually abuse children have no discursive space; they are in this sense socially excluded. They are occasionally included in the child-abuse discourse as colluders, male coerced, or psychiatrically disturbed, and for the professionals involved, this may present as an opportunity to minimise the behaviour. Female offenders who cannot be readily positioned within these categories remain outside the child-abuse dialogues. The concern here is that if there is not a place for discussing such behaviour, then we not only fail and silence these women but we fail and silence their victims as well. Clearly, the time and place is not yet right for the female paedophile to tell her story publicly—there is no-one ready to listen—but maybe we could begin by providing the opportunity for all women to discuss ambiguities in relationships with their children. While initiating such a discourse may be a meagre move towards protection, it could act as a catalyst for more in-depth narratives to emerge about the subtle and sensual relationships between women and children.

SOCIAL CONCEPTIONS OF WOMEN AND MOTHERING

The second underlying factor concerning the denial of female sexual abusers is our interpretation of what it is to be a woman and a mother and how this effects our perception of the behaviour. Motz has suggested that we need to readjust our understanding of the maternal role in order to accommodate female abusive behaviour: 'Understanding the female sexual offender requires the capacity to suspend social stereotypes about 'maternal instincts' and the ability to hear, from the offender herself, the story of her own mothering' (Motz 2001, 57).

There are two important social aspects about women in general that appear to be related to the response of denial and minimisation by female perpetrators: the assumption of women as victims and the social importance of the mothering role.

The Assumption of Women as Victims

We have discussed a number of problems connected to the notion of women as victims. Of course, not all female offenders are perceived as victims; some are just not the right type because they display various nonfeminine behaviours. But those women who appear to fit the ideal type can easily be displaced from the role of perpetrator to the role of victim, as we have seen within Chapter 3. For example, the account of the lawyer, who, despite knowing the mother had been sexually abusive towards her children, excused her behaviour. She was seen as a victim rather than a perpetrator.

Delia, in the same chapter, suggested that for those treating and counselling offenders the transposition is even more likely. Counsellors sometimes focus more readily on the victimisation suffered rather than the offending behaviour, as Delia found with her client Mary. For some abusers, this may be an unconscious denial; however, here we have a situation whereby the offender can choose to use the concept of victimisation as a rationale. It could become the perfect excuse, which releases them from the responsibility of sexually abusing children and aligns comfortably with the notions of both women as victims and the cycle of abuse theory.

Social Importance of Mothering

The social structure of motherhood and the mothering role have a significant bearing on the way female perpetrators are perceived. Mothers, and women generally, have a licence to be intimate with children in a way not available to most men. Within the course of everyday care, they touch, caress, and clean children, performing intimate tasks that would be considered at least sensual, if not overtly sexual, in any other context. Mothers have control over their children within the privacy of the family that is not usually questioned and professionals, especially those from welfare agencies, and they stress the importance of the mothering role, sometimes dictating the terms of that role. Both the family courts and criminal courts may well view the 'good enough' mother with more leniency than other women, this further emphasizes the importance of the maternal role. This book has shown how female perpetrators may adapt the professional idealisation of the mothering role as a technique of neutralisation, in order to form a socially acceptable rationale. We observed this in women like Janet, who rationalised her abusive behaviour as overenthusiastic child care.

We have to find ways that allow us to recognise that most women who sexually abuse children are culpable for their actions and need to accept responsibility. In order to achieve this, we need to move our analysis of such behaviour away from the social structures that have constrained our ideas, away from the essentialist approach and notions of coercion and victimisation. Of course, we have to recognise the limitations of choice available to women, so any framework for analysis needs to include the social context and relevant social structures. But if we fail, then we are faced with a situation that places the blame onto child victims and past history.

UNDERSTANDING DENIAL

From the discussion in Chapter 3, we can see that some professionals appear to align the behaviour of female perpetrators to fit their own image of feminine stereotypes. The gender assumptions that still permeate the professional work ideology exacerbate the problem, as illustrated by the comments from one social-work manager: 'A lot of men still think having sex with a young male or female is OK . . . they don't think of it as abuse . . . there is a professional acceptance that it happens.' As far as the female perpetrator is concerned, she added,

> But this (sexually abusive behaviour) has never been explored to my knowledge for women, so it doesn't happen. And maybe it doesn't to a great extent . . . we don't know . . . whether their behaviour is actually different or whether their behaviour is accepted in a funny sort of way, I don't know.

Thus, dealing with female perpetrators may in some ways fall outside professional guidelines. Consequently, some child-protection workers may appear to fall back on personal bias and stereotypes to inform practice. Or maybe to suggest 'it doesn't happen here' is just less complicated. For some, the only way that women's violent behaviour can be interpreted, other than in terms of the mad or male coerced, is if it can be minimised as normal (Ballinger 2000). Hence, the tendency of professionals, and female perpetrators themselves, is to normalise the behaviour of some women as an extension of mothering rather than as intentionally violent or sexual behaviour.

Where the evidence is overwhelming, some women, as we have seen, still have their stories minimised or rationalised in a variety of ways. This colludes with the offender, enabling her to construct a rationale of denial that hides the severity of the offence.

At first glance, more awareness training might be a way forward for some professionals; but in fact, where there is no real solution, child sexual abuse by women is easier to avoid or ignore. As raised earlier by Delia's remark, 'in a way increased awareness leads to more avoidance,' suggesting that some workers remain impotent when faced with the problem of female offenders regardless of knowledge base. Such a situation may be related to lack of resources, but nevertheless it is one that indicates the low level of harm and risk anticipated.

So, as in the case of professionals, we find that they may deny and minimise behaviour, deciding that women 'don't do it' unless they are male coerced, evil, mad, or malelike, and thus they offer explanations of the behaviour as overenthusiastic child care or misinterpretation of intent. When there is no other possibility, because the evidence is so obvious, then professionals may consider past victimisation to 'blame.' And this may in part be true but not usually an excuse acceptable for male offenders in the same circumstances. These responses highlight the limited professional experience in confronting female perpetrators, and the lack of theoretical development means that policy and practice tend to focus on the male offender. Furthermore, as there is little opportunity or encouragement to discuss any emotional discomfort, such behaviour arouses creates a more urgent need to ignore or deny any sexual abuse committed by a woman.

From the child victim's perspective, the position may appear more urgent. The way that paedophiles, including incest offenders, groom children to become coconspirators in the abuse leaves the victim with feelings of responsibility and guilt. For instance, Penny, in Chapter 4, expressed her feelings of guilt and responsibility for the sexual abuse that she suffered. The problems concerning maternal-incest victims may be even more acute, since not only is this something that women 'don't do' when mothers are involved it 'goes against nature.' The denial that faces victims should they choose to disclose just adds to their dilemmas, as shown by Louise, who thought that the other adults in her life should recognise the abuse she was suffering. While these child victims may feel unable to tell anyone of their pain, many of them, except the very young, developed resistance through some escape mechanisms, whether that is through dissociation or physical avoidance.

Of course, for victims the situation is different, but there is still a sense of denial, at least about the intent of the sexual behaviour. Reasons for this response may vary, dependent upon the age and sex of the child, but it would appear that some victims in cases of maternal incest have an urge to defend their mothers. So, for instance, the need to maintain the maternal-figure relationships with their mothers remained well into adulthood. And individuals like Dennis and Louise were still rationalising and excusing the behaviour of their mothers as well as demonstrating their desire to retain the relationship. Some male victims adopt a more aggressively masculine front, which suggests the need to maintain control and sexual intent. The relationship between Dennis and his neighbour might be an example of this and the way in which such feelings can feed into the denial and rationalisation of abuse.

Challenging the linear approach, we have to understand childhood, and perhaps moving away from a protectionist, welfare approach may offer children more rights and control over their lives. It may also mean that children have a more open environment within which to feel safe and disclose if they wish. The problems that could remain relate to the social expectations that the child has of the maternal relationship. After all, mothers are offered enormous 'power to validate the loveableness and value of children . . . mother can convince the world that we are worthwhile . . . mother can convince us of that . . . abused children want it' (Rosencrans 1997, 33).

We have considered a variety of rationales used by women, and the important point is that these explanations are formulated to deliver just what the audience expect. We have found a category of denials, justifications, and excuses that paedophiles recognise as fitting the social norm. For instance, the overenthusiastic child care suggested by Janet—'I had to get them clean'—adopts a mothering-skills approach. Margaret suggested a one-off mistake while under the influence of alcohol that pathologises and yet at the same time paradoxically normalises the behaviour. There are other acceptable rationales developing within the explanations of 'I felt he was mine' and 'I wanted to show him I loved him' that Brenda used. These just seem to extend the attributes of mothering that are so admired and desired within the ideal mother-child bond.

The vocabularies of motive that Margaret developed are familiar, for they have been used by male offenders. Being drunk, suggesting it only happened once, and blaming the victim are familiar justifications voiced by men accused of sexually abusing children. However, the motives suggested by Brenda and Janet include some very specific excuses that strike a chord with the current welfare emphasis on maternal bonding and good-enough mothering. It may be that these themes are offering a range of choice in terms of vocabularies of motive not available to male abusers.

Obviously the female offenders will deny any abuse or intent to harm, especially in the case of their own children. However, the rationale that they use offers us an insight into how they see their worlds and what they expect others to accept from women.

THE WAY FORWARD

Perhaps one way forward is to consider ways in which female perpetrators could become included in the academic discourse. There has been some notable comment about the absence of feminist theory in connection with women who commit violent and sexual crimes (Cameron 1999; Denov 2004; Motz 2001). Nevertheless, feminist theory has offered a considerable and valuable critique to sociology and criminology in terms of understanding sex crime, the male offender and the female victim. Feminists have also worked on opportunities for victims to speak out as well as challenging the male-steam focus of criminal justice. However, it is difficult to adapt this approach to female perpetrators, especially those who act alone, because the theory relies on patriarchy and the subordination of women. We need to question the stereotypes of masculinity and femininity more actively, and this would move us away from women as victims and men as aggressors. Some of this work has already begun (Renzetti 1999; Smart 1995; Worrall 2002), but there is more to do. And while the notion of women as victims may create problems for the recognition of female abusers, the concept of male aggression causes difficulties for male victims that we need to resolve. Male victimisation can easily remain invisible and cause confusion for individuals concerning their 'maleness' (Mendel 1995). More important is the resulting confusion between masculine expectations and the legacy of vulnerability left by abuse, which may be exhibited as anger. As some studies (Groth 1979; Petrovich and Templar 1984) have shown, the aftermath of sexual abuse by women may well be a significant factor in the behaviour of rapists.

The other issue concerning masculinity and femininity that needs some consideration is the understanding of difference. Not just the difference between men and women but the different masculinities and femininities that present and how these various groups and individuals are positioned within society. For instance, it would be wrong to imagine that all female perpetrators are the same. They do not all commit the same acts and the motivations may vary. Hearn (1988) suggested one of the questions we could consider in connection with male abusers is why some men do not use violence. In terms of the female offender, we could give some thought to why there are so few.

Another important factor is to ensure that a gender analysis is prominent, for women who act violently are not just women acting like men (Renzetti 1999). No matter how malelike the deviant behaviour, 'a woman within such a culture could not be in exactly the same position as a man' (Cameron 1999, 71). So we cannot simply assess women's violence from a male perspective (Messerschmidt 1997).

It is the child victims who can lose out the most if we ignore any sexual abuse by women. In many cases, they have been grossly abused and betrayed by women and some by their mothers, as well as being let down by the official system charged with protecting them. A useful question to consider is 'Why don't they tell?' Their stories appear to suggest two reasons: the fear of not being believed and the fear of losing the maternal figure. While the latter reason may be connected to a psychological bond, the social emphasis on what mothers, and women in general, are and how they behave with children has a large part to play. Alongside the mother-child relationship is the further difficulty of admitting that your mother uses you as a sex object—seeks satisfaction from your body.

The victims discussed in Chapter 4 all had difficulty in disclosing their stories. Some thought their story was too abusive to be heard by other adults, even those they loved and trusted. Other victims thought no-one would believe their abuser was their mother. The emphasis on the mother and her role and the expressed desire for a mother-child relationship was highlighted in the victims' stories. Louise was a prime example of this when she said, 'I cried for me mum, but not the mum I got.'

The difficulties of coming to terms with maternal incest and the socially acceptable relationship between mother and child have had long-term implications for all the victims. And sometimes problems continued even after the mother's death. May is still seeking explanations: 'I wish I could sever the links between me and my mother. Now I want to know more about her . . . what was her story and why. It won't excuse anything but it might make it easier to understand' (May). She had other things to say about the difficulties of coming to terms with maternal incest.

> All sexually abused children think in some ways, particularly if it's a
> parent, that they have done something wrong to deserve the abuse . . .
> the problem is if you have been sexually abused by your mother you
> can't discard her entirely. Apart from anything else she carried you in

her womb and delivered you . . . so you are inextricably linked together, whether you like it or not. Trying to deal with this . . . is very
difficult. (May)

How can we challenge the situations for child victims? We could move away
from the protectionist approach that has failed many victims and find alternative ways to develop resilience and competence in children. This is far from
perfect, and the problem of the private crime scene within the family will
always give adults a position of power. However, as this book has shown,
children who are victims of abuse do seek ways to resist adult power, and if
an escape route can be provided then they will find it. In some cases, Child-
Line has proved to be one way forward, for such an initiative gives power to
children in an environment of confidentiality so that they can remain anony-
mous while working through various options and coping strategies. Thus,
the victim can disclose abuse without fear of instantly losing a parent or
being removed from the family. Research (Weldon 1988) has suggested that
child victims who have a trusted adult or older sibling to talk to will fare
better in later life. ChildLine or similar organisations may be one answer to
the future of child protection, especially as this initiative empowers children
and ensures their rights are upheld. No matter how effective these initiatives
are, we are still confronted with the very young child, perhaps preverbal,
who suffers abuse. Some of the victims in this book have stories of abuse
that began at a very young age, which is important for challenging the way
we view the mothering role and the idealisation of the mother figure.

Women who sexually abuse children are the antithesis of current models
of femininity and the maternal, but it is sometimes easier for all concerned
if we imagine that this behaviour is a misunderstanding of the boundaries
of child care. The fact is that the behaviour committed by these offenders
was sexual.

Brenda penetrated her son John with objects and she masturbated her
other son, Charles.

Janet masturbated her partner's son.

Margaret digitally penetrated her granddaughter.

In order to achieve a socially acceptable status, these female offenders
have to find ways to realign their behaviour with social norms to develop
appropriate rationales. We can draw links between the understanding that
offenders have of socially acceptable norms and denial by highlighting the
ways in which behaviour is rationalised. What this uncovers is the techniques of neutralisation used that are voiced within the vocabularies of
motive. The ways in which female sexual abuse is denied, minimised, and
rationalised may hold the key to specific social-role constraints that need to
be challenged.

Appendix

This appendix offers a very brief background of the survivors and perpetrators in this book.

THE SURVIVORS—THE INTERVIEWS

Penny was born in 1939, just before war broke out. She suffered sexual and emotional abuse at the hands of her mother from about the age of two. The sexual abuse halted when she reached puberty, but the emotional abuse continued until her mother died.

Petra was 39 years old when I interviewed her. She was sexually abused by her mother and her father from the age of three. The sexual abuse she suffered at the hands of her mother stopped when she was about fourteen years old. Her father's abusive behaviour stopped when she took a student year abroad.

Louise was born in 1959. She was sexually and physically abused by her mother from an 'early age' until she was sixteen, when she went to live with her boyfriend and his parents.

May was born in 1948. Her mother sexually abused her from infancy until she was five years old. She was then sexually abused by her brother, his friend, and his friend's father.

Dennis was born in 1963. He suffered physical, emotional, and sexual abuse at the hands of his mother from an early age until he was put into residential care at the age of thirteen. He was then sexually abused by a female neighbour from the age of fourteen on his weekend visits home.

Alice and I communicated by letter and tape, as she did not want to meet. She never revealed her age. She was sexually abused by her mother from infancy.

Celia was born in 1944. She suffered emotional and physical abuse from both her mother and her father. She was seduced and sexually abused by her female music teacher when she was fourteen.

Jeff was sexually abused by a female friend of his mother's from the age of five years until he was about twelve.

MOTHER OF A SURVIVOR

Fiona lost custody of her children because she was in an open lesbian relationship. Her youngest daughter, Cheryl, was sexually abused by her stepmother, Shirley, when she was two years old.

THE OFFENDERS

Margaret was born in 1944. Margaret digitally penetrated her granddaughter. She was convicted of sexually abusing her eleven-year-old granddaughter Lisa and sentenced to two years' imprisonment. It is likely that she had been abusing Lisa for some time and that she had abused her own daughters when they were children.

Janet was born in 1958. Janet masturbated her partner's son. She was convicted of sexually abusing her partner's son and sentenced to nine months' imprisonment. The police suspected that she had sexually abused her own two children as well as her partner's daughter, but there was insufficient evidence to take this to criminal court.

Brenda was forty-four at the time of her interview. Brenda penetrated her son John with objects, and she masturbated her other son, Charles. She has never been convicted for the sexual abuse of her two sons, Charles and John. Brenda's behaviour was identified when she attended therapy sessions.

Andrea was a child minder who took pornographic pictures of and was photographed by a ten-year-old girl, Daisy.

Beth took pornographic pictures of her two young sons.

Jane, with others, sexually abused her young son Tim and her daughter over a period of five years.

Mary was sexually abused by her mother and went on to sexually abuse her own daughter.

Sophie encouraged her children to watch her having sex with her partner and to watch pornographic videos.

Deena sexually abused both of her young sons.

Notes

NOTES TO THE INTRODUCTION

1. Rape Crisis is a voluntary organisation with centres throughout the United Kingdom. They offer a number of services to victims, including telephone helpline, face-to-face counselling services, support groups, and court advocacy.
2. ChildLine is a free and confidential twenty-four-hour helpline for children and young people. It is a registered UK charity and was set up in 1986.
3. Sexual grooming—Ways used by perpetrators to gain trust and confidence of children, including through the internet, for their own purposes and sexual gratification.
4. For more information about the role of the media in creating moral panics, see Stanley Cohen, *Folk Devils and Moral Panic* (London: McGibbon and Kee, 1972), and the subsequent critique by A. McRobbie and S. Thornton 'Rethinking moral panic for multi-mediated social worlds,' *British Journal of Sociology* 46, no.4 (1995): 559–74.
5. As Jenks (1996) has pointed out, this overlooks the fact that 'the family is one of the most dangerous places for children to live in' (p. 91).
6. Kidscape is a national charity working for the protection of children. The First National Conference on Female Sexual Abuse organised by Kidscape in 1992 was lobbied by feminists, causing one speaker to withdraw.
7. Estela Welldon is a clinical psychologist who has worked therapeutically with female perpetrators over a considerable number of years. Her book *Mother, Madonna, Whore* was published in 1988. It was one of the first books in the United Kingdom offering recognition of female perpetrators.
8. The Sexual Offences Act is discussed in more detail in chapter 2.
9. Plummer (1995) talks about memories on a number of different levels, such as community memory and personal memory. So 'memories may be more than just the properties of individuals. There is also *social memory*' (p. 41).
10. L. Williams (1995) found that in cases where child sexual abuse was violent enough to be recorded in hospital records, thirty-eight percent of the adult women she subsequently interviewed did not remember the abuse. This rather refutes the suggestion that repressed memories are false.
11. Plummer (1995) recognised that very few paedophiles manage to tell their stories: 'once caught their own story goes silent ' (p. 118).

NOTES TO CHAPTER 2

1. Rosencrans's (1997) study of women abused by their mothers reveals a list of behaviours including: 'playing with my hair; giving me unwanted sexy night-gowns; playing with my fingers and putting her arm around me.'

2. The Cleveland enquiry has become symbolic in the history of child protection within the UK (Kitzinger 2004). It occurred in 1987, when 121 children from 57 families were taken into care, having been diagnosed as sexually abused. There was a high-profile media coverage of the disagreements between professionals and the claims of innocence of the parents. Any questions of malpractice were vindicated within the enquiry—although not necessarily in the media. And 'contrary to media myth most of the cases were "cleared" by the courts, most of the children became subjects of some form of state support or protection' (Campbell 1988, 1).

3. Victoria Climbie was an eight-year-old girl living in the UK with her great aunt. She was murder by her aunt and her aunt's boyfriend in 2000. She had 126 separate injuries on her body at the time of her death. The subsequent enquiry by Lord Laming cited poor interagency working and supervision and inadequate training as prime causes of the lack of protection offered to Victoria. Although some researchers feel that there were other underlying causes concerning the fears and emotional responses of the professionals involved with Victoria. These were not investigated or examined in the enquiry (Ferguson 2004; Dale et al. 2005). For the recommendations see *The Victoria Climbie Inquiry,* http://www.victoria-climbie-inquiry.org.uk/finreport/htm

4. For more information, see Helen Walters, *An Introduction to Child Protection Legislation in the UK* (2007).

5. Within the Children Acts (2004, 1989) there is the requirement to assess the risk of harm to the child or children at the centre of a child-protection concern. If there is a risk of 'significant harm,' then there is a duty placed on professionals to seek the leave of the family courts to remove the child. The Common Assessment Framework offers some guidance in the measurement of 'significant harm' and there is an onus on professionals from various disciplines to work together in order to make these decisions.

6. *Looked after* is a term used for children who are cared for away from home by social services.

7. The guardian ad litem is independent of the court to ensure that the views and opinions of the child are accounted for.

8. Emergency Protection Order, see 1989 Children Act s. 44–5

9. These were introduced to ensure a common risk assessment of children in need and a clear line of responsibility within the safeguarding boards. For more information about the common assessment framework and Safeguarding Children Boards, see the government publications *Every Child Matters,* http://www.everychildmatters.gov.uk/.

10. It is difficult to prosecute when child victims are very young and there is inadequate corroborating evidence. In cases where young children are involved, it is usually up to the judge to decide whether they are able to be suitable witnesses or not.

11. See recommendations made within the Youth and Criminal Justice Act 1999, such as witness protection, screens in court, judges not wearing wigs and gowns, television links, and video evidence.

12. See the Home Office publication *Setting the Boundaries: Reforming the Law on Sex Offences,* July 2000.

13. Sexual grooming—ways used by perpetrators to gain the trust and confidence of children, including through the Internet, for their own purposes

14. The Sexual Offences Act (2003) considers that only men can be physically capable of rape—although women may be considered as accessories to the act.
15. For instance, the new sexual offences law recognises that both men and women can commit incest and other sexual offences against children (other than rape) and are liable under the same tariff of punishment.
16. See Chapter 3 for an analysis of professionals accounts.
17. For instance, the Cleveland affair—see DHSS (1988), 'Report of the Enquiry into Child Abuse,' HMSO.
18. The 'good enough' mother is a very subjective notion. Winnicott (1964) refers to the 'maternal environment' in which most mothers 'naturally' respond to their children. Chodorow (1978), within her interpretation of object-relations theory, considers the social construction of the mother-infant relationship. For more analysis, see Doane and Hodges (1992).
19. For useful discussion of constructions of culpability, see Barbara Hudson (2002).

NOTES TO CHAPTER 3

1. Professional closure is a term used by Witz (1992) to describe the activity of workers and their managers when they close ranks behind their professional procedures and practices and pass on, or bypass, the responsibility for a client.
2. This was also found to be the case in earlier work (Turner, 1995).
3. For example, one study (Taylor 1998, 57) found that 'in 1993 North Wales Police referred over 300 cases (to the crown prosecution service) of which less than 3 per cent proceeded . . .'
4. Rosemary West, the most prolific female serial killer in the UK, was convicted in 1995 of sexually assaulting and murdering 10 girls and young women, including her own daughter, her stepdaughter, and a pregnant lodger. Her husband Fred committed suicide before the trial.
5. See further discussion in Chapter 2.
6. It might be useful to explore this idea using some of the experience of attempting social inclusion for illegal drug users.
7. See Chapter 5.
8. See endnote 14, Chapter 2.
9. See example at beginning of chapter.
10. Several children's homes in the Gwynedd and Clwyd areas of Wales become a cause for concern following accusations by children and disclosures by adults who had been in care whilst young and the persistence of an employee—Alison Taylor—who was concerned about the treatment of children in care. The resulting inquiry covered a period of time from the mid-1970s to the late 1990s. A number of care staff were convicted of physical and sexual abuse against the children in their care. For more information, see Waterhouse (2000).

NOTES TO CHAPTER 4

1. See Jenks (1996) for a summary of these critiques.
2. A list of survivors and brief biographies can be found in appendix (i).
3. This was said to Penny as a child when she tried to tell an adult family friend about the abuse.

4. For discussion about perpetrators and denial, see Chapter 5.
5. It is not the focus of this work to explore concepts around the body in depth, but clearly many child-abuse victims have problems concerning their body image in connection with self-identity, sexuality, sensuality, and in relationship to the outside world. For further discussion, see Giddens (1991) and Foucault (1981); and for some more focussed thoughts on incest, see Bell (1993) and Gittens (1998).
6. Hunter (1993) relates the story of Lucy, whose mother tried to suffocate and strangle her because she did not comply with her wishes.

NOTES TO CHAPTER 5

1. The work of Gerth and Mills was developed from an earlier paper, 'Situated Actions and Vocabularies of Motive,' C. Wright Mills, *American Sociological Review* 1940, 5, 904–13.
2. A list of offenders and brief biographies can be found in appendix (i).
3. Taylor's (1972) paper was based on an analysis of male sexual deviants convicted of a variety of offences, including indecent exposure, indecent assault, and rape. None of these men, as far as we know, were child sexual abusers. Many of the justifications identified by Taylor were used as rationale by the female sexual abusers in this study.
4. A useful summary of concepts of denial, by Ruth Jamieson, in *Sage Dictionary of Criminology* (2001), London: Sage.
5. In this case, Andrea used grooming techniques that are often adopted by male paedophiles.
6. Taylor found in his study that male offenders suggested ' . . . a form of temporary insanity which rendered him incapable of distinguishing right from wrong' (1972, 29).
7. For details of some of these instances, see Carole Smart (1989) and Terry Thomas (2000).
8. See court cases cited in Carole Smart (1989).
9. Adapted from Taylor's (1972) *Defective Social Skills*, where the justification by male offenders was 'clumsiness with women.'
10. It was interesting to note how Janet sometimes adopted this use of 'professional jargon.' It added to her vocabulary of rationale and in the interview seemed to be used in a way to please the interviewer. Maybe she thought this is what I wanted to hear?
11. See case studies in Elliott (1993); Saradjian (1996); Rosencrans (1997).
12. This rationale was not identified by Taylor (1972). However, the element of ownership and control described here may also be relevant to male child abuser (Finkelhor 1984; Howitt 1995).
13. Taylor (1972) recognised this claim by male offenders as a way of legitimising sexual deviance as innovative, exciting sexual experience regardless of legal or moral social boundaries. A resistance to social norms maybe?
14. Such as single mothers, spinsters, surrogate mothers, childless women—see Smart (1995) for discussion on these 'dangerous' women.
15. Brenda was sexually abused by her father and one of her brothers. Some of her adult partnerships have also been abusive.
16. Taylor's (1972) work found some male offenders referred to themselves as 'sex mad.'

References

Allen, C. 1990. Women as perpetrators of child sexual abuse: Recognition barriers. In A. Horton et al., eds., *Incest perpetrators: A family member no-one wants to treat*. CA: Sage Focus.
———. 1991. *Women and men who sexually abuse children: A comparative analysis*. London: Safer Society Press.
Anderson, K., and D. Jack. 1991. Learning to listen. In S. Gluck and D. Patai, eds., *Women's words*. New York: Routledge.
Aptheker, B. 1989. *Tapestries of life: Women's work, women's consciousness and the meaning of daily experience*. USA: University of Massachusetts Press.
Araji, S., and D. Finkelhor. 1986. Abusers: A review of the research. In D. Finkelhor and Associates, *A sourcebook on child sexual abuse*. CA: Sage .
Aries, P. 1962. *Centuries of childhood: A social history of family life*. London: Cape.
Armstrong, L. 1978. *Kiss daddy goodnight*. New York: Hawthorn.
———. 1990. Making an issue out of incest. In D. Leidholdt and J. Raymond, eds., *The sexual liberals and the attack on feminism*. New York: Pergamon Press.
———. 1994. *Rocking the cradle of sexual politics: What happened when women said incest?* USA: Addison-Wesley.
Asquith, S. 1993. *Protecting children. Cleveland to Orkney: More lessons to learn?* Edinburgh: HMSO.
Bacon, H., and S. Richardson. 2000. Child sexual abuse and the continuum of victim disclosure: Professionals working with children in Cleveland in 1987. In C. Itzin, ed., *Home truths about child sexual abuse*. London: Routledge.
Balint M, 1965. *Primary love and psychoanalytic technique*, London, UK, Tavistock Publications
Ballinger, A. 2000. *Dead woman walking: Executed women in England and Wales 1900–1955*. Aldershot, UK: Ashgate.
Banning, A. 1989. Mother-son incest: Confronting the prejudice. *Child Abuse and Neglect*, 13, 563–570.
Barrett, R. 1996. *The psychiatric team and the social definition of schizophrenia*. New York: Cambridge Univ. Press.
Barrett, M., and M. McIntosh. 1991. *The anti-social family*, 2nd ed. London: Verso.
Beck, U. 1992. *Risk society: Towards a new modernity*. London: Sage.
Beck, U., and E. Beck-Gernsheim. 1995. *The normal chaos of love*. Cambridge, UK: Polity Press.
Bell, V. 1993. *Interrogating incest: Feminism, Foucault and the law*. London: Routledge.
———. 2003. The vigilant(e) parent and the paedophile: The News of the World campaign 2000 and the contemporary governmetality of child sexual abuse. In

P. Reavey and S.Warner, eds., *New feminist stories of child sexual abuse: Sexual scripts and dangerous dialogues.* London: Routledge.

Belsky, J. 1980. Child maltreatment: An ecological integration. *American Psychologist,* 35:320–400.

———. 1993. Etiology of child maltreatment: A developmental-ecological analysis. *Psychological Bulletin,* 114:413–34.

Benjamin, J. 1990. *The bonds of love.* London: Virago Press.

Birch, H. 1993. If looks could kill: Myra Hindley and the iconography of evil. In H. Birch, ed., *Moving Targets: Women, murder and representation.* London: Virago Press.

Bolen, R., D. Russell, and M. Scannapieco. 2000. The nature and extent of child sexual abuse. In C. Itzen, ed., *Home truths about child sexual abuse.* London: Routledge.

Boseley, S., (health editor), 12 July 2001. Youth seduced by older woman 'will suffer trauma in later life', *Guardian Unlimited,* http://www.guardian.co.uk/uk_news/story/0,,520325,00.html

Bowlby, J. 1965. *Child care and the growth of love.* London: Pelican Books.

———. 1988. *A secure base: Clinical applications of attachment theory.* London: Routledge.

Briere J and K. Smiljanich, August, 1993, *Childhood sexual abuse and subsequent sexual aggression against adult women,* Paper presented at the 101st annual convention of the American Psychological Association, Toronto, Canada

Brownmiller, S. 1981. *Against our will: Men, women and rape.* New York: Bantam.

Bryson, V. 1999. *Feminist debates: Issues of theory and political practice.* London: Macmillan.

Buchanan, A. 1996. *Cycles of child maltreatment: Facts, fallacies and interventions.* Chichester, UK: Wiley.

Bullock, R., M. Little, S. Millham, and K. Mount. 1995, *Child protection: messages form the research,* London, UK, HMSO

Bunting, L. 2005. *Females who sexually offend against children: Responses of the child protection and criminal justice systems.* London: NSPCC.

Burman, E. 2003. Childhood, sexual abuse and contemporary political subjectives. In P. Reavey and S. Warner, eds., *New feminist stories of child sexual abuse: Sexual scripts and dangerous dialogues.* London: Routledge.

Butler, I. 1996. Children and the sociology of childhood: A case of neglect. In I. Butler and I. Shaw, eds., *Children's experiences and the sociology of childhood.* UK: Avebury.

Butler, I., and H. Williamson. 1994. *Children speak: Children, trauma and social work.* UK: Longman.

Cain M, 1996. Towards transgression: new directions in feminist criminology, in J. Muncie, E. McLaughlin & M. Langan, eds., *Criminological Perspectives,* London, UK, Sage

Cameron, D. 1999. Rosemary West: Motives and meanings. *Journal of Sexual Aggression,* 4(2), 68–80.

Campbell, B. 1988. *Unofficial secrets, child sexual abuse—the Cleveland case.* London: Virago.

Carlen, P. 1990. *Alternatives to women's imprisonment.* Milton Keynes, UK: Oxford Univ. Press.

———. 2002. *Women and Punishment.* Devon, UK: Willan.

Carrabine, E., P. Cox, M. Lee, and N. South. 2002. *Crime in modern Britain.* London: Oxford Univ. Press.

Carrington, K. 2002. Feminism and critical criminology: Confronting genealogies. In K. Carrington and R. Hogg, eds., *Critical criminology: Issues, debates, challenges.* Devon, UK: Willan.

Cavanagh, J. T. 1989. Female child perpetrators: Children who molest other children. *Child Abuse and Neglect*, 13:571–85.

Chodorow, N. 1978. *The reproduction of mothering*. Berkeley: Univ. of California Press.

Chodorow, N., and S. Contratto. 1992. The fantasy of the perfect mother. In B. Thorne and M. Yalom, eds., *Re-thinking the family*. Boston: Northeastern Univ. Press.

Cobley, C. 1995. *Child abuse and the law*. London: Cavendish.

Cohen, S. 1993. Human rights and the crimes of the state: The culture of denial. In J. Muncie, E. McLaughlin, and M. Langan, eds., *Criminological perspectives (1996)*.

Buckingham, UK: Open Univ. Press.

———. 2001. *States of denial: Knowing about atrocities and suffering*. Cambridge, UK: Polity.

———. 2002. *Folk devils and moral panics*, 3rd ed. London: Routledge.

Coleman K, C. Hird, and D. Povey. 2006, *Violent crime overview, homicide and gun crime 2004/2005*, 2nd ed., (Supplementary volume to crime in England and Wales 2004/2005), Crown Copyright, UK, Home Office Statistical Bulletin

Connell, R. W. 1995. *Masculinities*. Cambridge, UK: Polity Press.

Cooper, A., R. Hetherington, and I. Katz. 2003. *The risk factor: Making the child protection system work for children*. London: Demos.

Cossins, A. 2000. Masculinities, sexualities and child sexual abuse. Cambridge, USA: Kluwer Law International.

Coward, R. 1997. The heaven and hell of mothering: Mothering and ambivalence in the mass media. In W. Hollway and B. Featherstone, eds., *Mothering and ambivalence*. London: Routledge.

Creighton, S. 2004. *Child protection statistics: Child deaths*, NSPCC Child Protection Research Group, NSPCC Inform, www.nspcc,org,uk/Inform.

Creighton, S., and G. Tissier. 2003. *Child killings in England and Wales*, NSPCC Research Department/NSPCC Media Office, NSPCC Inform, www.nspcc.org.uk/Inform

Dale, P., R. Green, and R. Fellows.2005. *Child protection assessment following serious injuries to infants: Fine judgments*. Chichester, Sussex, UK: Wiley.

Davin, P. 1999. Secrets revealed: A study of female sex offenders. In P. Davin, J. Hislop, and T. Dunbar, eds., *Female sexual abusers: Three views*, Brandon, VT: Safer Society Press.

Davin, P., J. Hislop, and T. Dunbar. 1999. *Female sexual abusers: Three views*. Brandon, VT: Safer Society Press.

Denov, M. 2004. *Perspectives on female sexual offending: A culture of denial*. UK: Ashgate.

Department of Health and Social Security (DHSS). 1988. *Report of the enquiry into child abuse Cleveland 1987*. London: HMSO.

DiQuinzio, P. 1999. *The impossibility of motherhood: Feminism, individualism and the problem of mothering*. New York: Routledge.

Doane, J., and D. Hodges. 1992. *From Klein to Kristeva: Psychoanalytic feminism and the search for the 'good enough' mother*. Ann Arbor: Univ. of Michigan Press.

Donzelot, J. 1980. *The policing of families*. London: Hutchinson.

Douglas, M. 1984. *Purity and Danger: An analysis of the concepts of pollution and taboo*. London: Ark Paperbacks.

———. 1992. *Risk and Blame: Essays in cultural theory*. London: Routledge.

Driver, E., and A. Droisen. 1989. *Child sexual abuse: Feminist perspectives*. Basingstoke, UK: Macmillan.

Dunbar, T. 1999. Women who sexually molest female children. In P. Davin, J. Hislop, and T. Dunbar, eds., *Female sexual abusers: Three views*. Brandon, VT: Safer Society Press.

Duncan, N. 1996. Renegotiating gender and sexuality in public and private spaces. In N. Duncan, ed., *Body space: Destabilizing geographies of gender and sexuality.* London: Routledge.

Duncombe J., and D. Marsden. 1998. "Stepford wives" and "hollow men": doing emotional work, doing gender and "authenticity" in intimate heterosexual relationships, in G. Bendelow and S.J. Williams, eds., *Emotions in social life: critical themes and contemporary issues,* London, UK, Routledge

Dworkin, A. 1981. *Pornography: Men possessing women.* London: The Women's Press.

Elliott, M. 1993. What survivors tell us: An overview. In M Elliott, ed., *The last taboo.* London: Longman.

Eldridge H, June, 1998. *Treatment and therapy,* Paper presented at National Study Day of the British Association for the Study and Prevention of Child Abuse and Neglect, Brighton, UK

Etherington, K. 1996. Maternal sexual abuse of males. *Child Abuse Review,* 6(10), 107–17.

Faller, K. 1987. Women who sexually abuse children. *Violence and Victims,* 2:4:263–76.

———. 1993. *Child sexual abuse: Intervention and treatment issues,* http://www.calib.com/nccanch/pubs/usermaunual/sexabuseindex.cfm.

Featherstone, B. 1996. Victims or villains? Women who physically abuse their children. In B. Fawcett et al., eds., *Violence and gender relations: Theories and interventions.* London: Sage.

———. 1997. Introduction: Crisis in the Western family. In W. Hollway and B. Featherstone, eds., *Mothering and ambivalence.* New York,: Palgrave Macmillan.

———. 2004. *Family life and family support: A feminist analysis.* London: Routledge.

Ferguson, H. 2004. *Protecting children in time: Child abuse, child protection and the consequences of modernity.* Hampshire, UK: Palgrave.

Finkelhor, D. 1983. Introduction. In D. Finkelhor et al., eds., *The dark side of families.* New York: Sage.

———. 1984. *Child sexual abuse: New theory and research.* New York: The Free Press.

———. 1986. *The trauma of child sexual abuse: Two models.* Concord: Univ. of New Hampshire.

———. 1993. The main problem is still under-reporting, not over-reporting. In R. J. Gelles and D. R. Loseke, eds., *Current controversies on family violence.* CA: Sage.

Finkelhor, D., & Associates. 1986b. *A sourcebook on child sexual abuse.* CA: Sage.

Finkelhor, D., L. Meyer-Williams, and N. Burns. 1988. *Nursery crimes: Sexual abuse in day care.* London: Sage.

Flavin, J., and A. Desautels. 2006. Feminism and crime. In C. Renzetti, L. Goodstein, and S. Miller, eds., *Rethinking gender, crime and justice: Feminist readings.* CA: Roxbury.

Forbes, J. 1992. Female sexual abusers: The contemporary search for equivalence. *Practice* 6(20), 102–11.

Ford, H. 2006. *Women who sexually abuse children.* Chichester, UK: Wiley.

Forna, A. 1998. *Mother of all myths: How society moulds and constrains mothers.* London: HarperCollins.

Foucault, M. 1981. *The history of sexuality,* vol. 1. London: Penguin.

———. 1977, *Discipline and punish: the birth of the prison,* translated from the French by A. Sheridan, London, UK, Allen Lane

Freund, K., R. J. Watson, and R. Dickey. 1990. Does sexual abuse in childhood cause pedophilia? An exploratory study. *Archives of Sexual Behaviour*, 19(6), 557–68.

Fromuth, M., and B. Burkhart. 1987. Childhood sexual victimization among college men: Definitional and methodological issues. *Violence and Victims*, 2(4), 241–53.

Gavey, N. 1999. "I wasn't raped, but . . .": Revisiting definitional problems in sexual victimization. In S. Lamb, ed., *New versions of victims: Feminists struggle with the concept*. New York: New York Univ. Press.

Gelles, R. J. 1993. Through a sociological lens: Social structure and family violence. In R. J. Gelles and D. R. Loseke, eds., *Current controversies on family violence*. CA: Sage.

Gelles, R. J., and D. R. Loseke. 1993. *Current controversies on family violence*. CA: Sage.

Gelsthorpe, L. 1990. Feminist methodologies in criminology: A new approach or old wine in new bottles? In L. Gelsthorpe and A. Morris, eds., *Feminist perspectives in criminology*. Buckingham, UK: Open Univ. Press.

Gerth, H., and C. Wright Mills. 1954. *Character and social structure*. London: Routledge & Kegan Paul.

Ghate, D., and L. Spencer. 1995. *The prevalence of child sexual abuse in Britain*. London: HMSO.

Giddens, A. 1991. *Modernity and self-identity: Self and society in the late modern age*. Cambridge, UK: Polity Press.

———. 1992. *The transformation of intimacy: Sexuality, love and eroticism in modern societies*. Stanford, CA: Stanford Univ. Press.

Gittens, D. 1993. *The family in question*. London: Macmillan.

———. 1998. *The child in question*. London: Macmillan.

Glaser, B. G., and A. L. Strauss. 1967. *The discovery of the grounded theory: Strategies for qualitative research*. Chicago: Aldine.

Glaser, D., and S. Frosh. 1988. *Child sex abuse*. London: Macmillan.

Glenn, E. 1994. Social constructions of mothering. In E. N. Glenn, G. Chang, and L. R. Forcey, eds., *Mothering: Ideology, experience and agency*. London: Routledge.

Goodwin, J., and P. Divasto. 1979. Mother-daughter incest. *Child Abuse and Neglect*, 3, 953–57.

Gordon, L. 1992. Family violence, feminism and social control. In B. Thorne and M. Yalom, eds., *Re-thinking the family*. Boston: Northeastern Univ. Press.

Gottfredson, M., and Hindelang, J. 1977. Consideration of telescoping and memory decay biases in victimization surveys. *Journal of Criminal Justice*, 5:3, 205–16.

Grayston, A., and R. De Luca. 1999. Female perpetrators of child sexual abuse: A review of the clinical and empirical literature. *Aggression and Violent Behaviour*, 4:1:93–06.

Green, L. 2001. Children, sexual abuse and the child protection system. In P. Foley, J. Roche, and S. Tucker, eds., *Children in society: Contemporary theory and practice*. Basingstoke, UK: Palgrave.

Groth, N. 1979. *Men who rape*. New York: Plenum.

———. 1984. The incest offender. In S. Sgroi, ed., *Handbook of clinical intervention in child sexual abuse*. Lexington, KY: Lexington Books.

Grubin, D. 1998. *Sex offending against children: Understanding the risk*. London: Police and Reducing Crime Unit, RDS.

Harding, S. 1987. *Feminism and methodology*. USA: Indiana Univ. Press/London: Open Univ. Press.

Hearn, J. 1988. Commentary. Child abuse: Violences and sexualities towards young people. *Sociology*, 22:4:531–44.

Hearn, J., and D. Morgan. 1990. *Men, masculinities and social theory.* London: Unwin Hyman Ltd.

Heidensohn, F. 1985. *Women and crime.* London: Macmillan.

Heritage, J. 1984. *Garfinkel and ethnomethodology.* Cambridge, UK: Polity Press.

Herman, J. 1981. *Father-daughter incest.* Cambridge, MA: Harvard Univ. Press.

Hetherton, J. 1999. The idealization of women: Its role in the minimization of child sexual abuse by females. *Child abuse and Neglect,* 23:2:161–74.

Hetherton, J., and L. Beardsall. 1998. Decisions and attitudes concerning child sexual abuse: Does the gender of the perpetrator make a difference to child protection professionals? *Child Abuse and Neglect,* 22:12:1265–83.

Hevey, D., and H. Kenward. 1989. The effects of child sexual abuse. In W. Stainton-Rogers, D. Hevey, and E. Ash, eds., *Child abuse and neglect.* London: Open Univ. Press.

Hislop, J. 1999. Female child molesters. In P. Davin, J. Hislop, and T. Dunbar, eds., *Female sexual abusers: Three views.* Brandon, VT: Safer Society Press.

———. 2001. *Female sex offenders: What therapists, law enforcement and child protective services need to know.* Ravensdale, USA: Issues Press.

H.M. Government. 2006. *Working together to safeguard children: A guide to inter-agency working to safeguard and promote the welfare of children,* http://www.everychildmatters.gov.uk/resources-and-practice/IG00060/.

H.M. Stationery Office (HMSO). 1988. *Working together: A guide to arrangements for inter-agency co-operation for the protection of children from abuse.* London.

———. 1995. *Child protection: Messages from research.* London.

Hobbs, C., and J. Wynne. 1994, The Leeds experience, in V. Sinason, ed., *Treating survivors of satanist abuse,* London, UK, Routledge

Hollaway, W. 1997. The maternal bed. In W. Hollway and B. Featherstone, eds., *Mothering and ambivalence.* London: Routledge.

Holmes, J. 1993. *John Bowlby and attachment theory.* London: Routledge.

Home Office. 2000. *Setting the boundaries: Reforming the law on sex offences.* London: Home Office Communications Directorate.

———. 2002. *Protecting the public, strengthening protection against sex offenders and reforming the law on sexual offences, CM 5668.* London: The Stationery Office.

———. 2003. *Statistics on women and the criminal justice system: A Home Office publication under section 95 of the Criminal Justice Act 1991.* London: Research, Development and Criminal Statistics Division, Home Office.

hooks, b. 1981. *Ain't I a woman: Black women and feminism.* Boston: South End Press.

Hooper, C. 1992. Child sexual abuse and the regulation of women: Variations on a theme. In C. Smart, ed., *Regulating womanhood.* London: Routledge

Howe, D. 2005. *Child abuse and neglect: Attachment, development and intervention.* London: Palgrave Macmillan.

Howitt, D. 1995. *Paedophiles and sexual offences against children.* Chichester, UK: Wiley.

Hudson, A. 1992. The child sexual abuse 'industry' and gender relations in social work. In M. Langan and L. Day, eds., *Women, oppression and social work.* London: Routledge.

Hudson, B. 2002. Gender issues in penal policy. In P. Carlen, ed., *Women and punishment.* Devon, UK: Willan.

Hunt, G. 1998. Why does it go on and on? In G. Hunt, ed., *Whistleblowing in the social services: Public accountability and professional practice.* London: Arnold.

Hunt, J., A. Macleod, and C. Thomas. 1999. *The last resort: Child protection, the courts and the 1989 Children Act.* London: The Stationery Office.

Hunter, K. 1993. Helping survivors through counseling. In M. Elliott, ed., *Female sexual abuse of children: The ultimate taboo.* Harlow, UK: Longmans.

James, A., C. Jenks, and A. Prout. 1998. *Theorising childhood.* Cambridge, UK: Polity Press.

Jefferson, T. 1996. The James Bulger case: A review essay. *British Journal of Criminology,* 36:2:319–23.

Jenkins, P. 1998. *Moral panic: Changing concept of the child molester in modern America.* New Haven, CT: Yale Univ. Press.

Jenks, C. 1996. *Childhood.* London: Routledge.

Justice, B., and R. Justice. 1979. *The broken taboo.* New York: Human Sciences.

Kaufman, K., A. Wallace, C. Johnson, and M. Reeder. 1995. Comparing female and male perpetrators'modus operandi. *Journal of Interpersonal Violence,* 10:3:322–33.

Kelly, L. 1988. *Surviving sexual violence.* Cambridge, UK: Polity.

———. 1996. When does the speaking profit us?: Reflections on the challenges of developing feminist perspectives on abuse and violence by women. In M. Hester, L. Kelly, and J. Radford, eds., *Women, violence and male power: Feminist activism, research and practice.* Buckingham, UK: Open Univ. Press.

———. 1997a. Weasel words: Paedophiles and the cycle of abuse. *NOTA News,* 22, 9–19.

———. 1997b. A central issue: Sexual violence and feminist theory. In S. Kemp and J. Squires, eds., *Feminisms.* Oxford, UK: Oxford Univ. Press.

Burton, S., L. Kelly, L. Regan, and R. Wingfield. 1995. *Splintered lives: Sexual exploitation of children in the context and of children's rights and child protection.* Ilford, UK: Barnardo's.

Kitzinger, J. 1988. Defending Innocence: Ideologies of childhood. *Feminist Review,* 28, 77–87.

———. 1997. Who are you kidding? Child, power, and the struggle against sexual abuse, In A. James and A. Prout, eds., *Constructing and reconstructing childhood.* London: Routledge Falmer.

———. 2004. *Framing abuse: Media influences and public understanding of sexual violence against children.* London: Pluto Press.

Koonin, R. 1995. Breaking the last taboo: Child sex abuse by female perpetrators. *Australian Journal of Social Issues,* 3, 195–210.

Kvale, S. 1996. *Interviews: An introduction to qualitative research interviewing.* Beverly Hills, CA: Sage Focus.

La Fountaine, J. 1990. *Child sexual abuse.* Cambridge, UK: Polity Press.

———. 1998. *Speak of the devil: Tales of satanic abuse in contemporary England.* Cambridge, UK: Cambridge Univ. Press.

Lamb, S. 1996. *The trouble with blame: Victims, perpetrators and responsibility.* New Haven, CT: Harvard Univ. Press.

———. 1999. Constructing the victim: Popular images and lasting labels. In S. Lamb, ed., *New versions of victims: Feminists struggle with the concept.* New York: New York Univ. Press.

Laming, Lord. 2003. *The Victoria Climbie Inquiry,* http://www.victoria-climbie-inquiry.org.uk/finreport/htm.

Langford, W. 1996. Romantic love and power. In T. Cosslett, A. Easton, and P. Summerfield, eds., *Women power and resistance: An introduction to women's studies.* Buckingham, UK: Open Univ. Press.

Lansdown, G. 2001. Children's welfare and children's rights. In P. Foley, J. Roche, and S. Tucker, eds., *Children in society: Contemporary theory and practice.* Basingstoke, UK: Palgrave.

Lawler, S. 1996. Motherhood and identity. In T. Cosslett, A. Easton, and P. Summerfield, eds., *Women, power and resistance: An introduction to women's studies.* Buckingham, UK: Open Univ. Press.

Lawrence, A. 2004. *Principles of child protection: Management and practice.* Maidenhead, UK: Open Univ. Press.

Lawson, C. 1993. Mother-son sexual abuse: Rare or underreported? A critique of the research. *Child Abuse and Neglect,* 17(2), 261–69.

Lee, R., and C. Renzetti. 1993. The problems of researching sensitive topics. In C. Renzetti and R. Lee, eds., *Researching sensitive topics.* Beverly Hills, CA: Sage Focus.

Leidholdt, D., and J. Raymond. 1990. *The sexual liberals and the attack on feminism.* New York: Pergamon.

Liddle, A. M. 1993. Gender, desire and child sexual abuse: Accounting for the male majority. *Theory, Culture and Society,* 10:103–26.

Loader, I. 1996. *Youth, policing and deviancy.* Basingstoke, UK: Macmillan.

Lyman, S., and M. Scott. 1970. *A sociology of the absurd.* CA: Goodyear.

Matthews, J., R. Mathews, and K. Speltz. 1991. Female sexual offenders: A typology. In M. Quinn Patton, ed., *Family sexual abuse, frontline research and evaluation.* Newbury Park, CA: Sage.

Mathews, R., J. Matthews, and K. Speltz. 1989. Female sexual offenders: An exploratory study. Brandon, VT: Safer Society Press.

Mathis, J. 1972. *Clear thinking about sexual deviations.* Chicago: Nelson-Hall.

Mauthner, N., and A. Doucet. 1998. Reflections on a voice-centred relational method: Analysing maternal and domestic voices. In J. Ribbens and R. Edwards, eds., *Feminist dilemmas in qualitative research.* London: Sage.

McCaghy, C. 1968. Drinking and deviance disavowel: The case of child molesters. *Social Problems,* 16, 43–49.

McIntosh, M. 1988. Family secrets as public drama. *Feminist Review, Family Secrets,* 28, 6–16.

McKinnon, S. 1995. American kinship/American incest: Asymmetries in a scientific discourse. In S. Yanagisako and C. Delaney, eds., *Naturalising power.* London: Routledge.

McLaughlin, E. 2001. Political violence, terrorism and states of fear. In J. Muncie and E. McLaughlin, eds., *The problem of crime,* 2nd ed. Buckingham, UK: Open Univ. Press.

Mendel, M. 1995. *The male survivor: The impact of sexual abuse.* Beverly Hills, CA: Sage Focus.

Mendes, P. 2000. Social conservatism versus social justice: The portrayal of child abuse in Victoria, Australia. *Child Abuse Review,* 9, 49–61.

Messerschmidt, J. 1997. *Crime as structured action: Gender, race, class and crime in the making.* CA: Sage.

Miletski, H. 1995. *Mother-son incest: The unthinkable broken taboo.* Brandon, VT: Safer Society Press.

Miller, A. 1987. *The drama of being a child.* London: Virago Press.

Miller, T. 1998. Shifting layers of professional, lay and personal narratives: Longitudinal childbirth research. In J. Ribbens and R. Edwards, eds., *Feminist dilemmas in qualitative research.* London: Sage.

Minister, K. 1991. A feminist framework for the oral history interview. In S. Gluck and D. Patai, eds., *Women's words.* New York: Routledge.

Mitra, C., 1987. Judicial discourse in father-daughter incest appeal cases, *International Journal of the Sociology of Law,* 15:2:121-48

Morgan, D. H. J. 1996. *Family connections.* Cambridge, UK: Polity Press.

Morris, A., and A. Wilcznski. 1993. Rocking the cradle: Mothers who kill their children. In H. Birch, ed., *Moving targets: Women, murder and representation.* London: Virago Press.

Morrison, T. 1997. Emotionally competent child protection organisations: Fallacy, fiction or necessity? In J. Bates, R. Pugh, and N. Thompson, eds., *Protecting children: Challenges and change.* Aldershot, UK: Arena.

Morss, J. 1996. *Growing critical: Alternatives to developmental psychology.* London: Routledge.

Motz, A. 2001. *The psychology of female violence: Crimes against the body.* Hove, UK: Brunner-Routledge.

Nakano, G. E. 1994. Social Constructions of mothering: Athematic overview. In G. E. Nakano, G, Chang, L. Rennie Forcey, eds., *Mothering: Ideology, experience and agency.* New York: Routledge.

Nasjleti, M. 1980. Suffering in silence: The male incest victim. *Child Welfare, LIX* (5), 269–75.

Nelson, E. D. 1994. Females who sexually abuse children: A discussion of gender stereotypes and symbolic assailants. *Qualitative Sociology,* 17:1:63–88.

Nelson, S. 1998. *The body keeps the score: The dangerousness of evidence on physical effects of child sexual abuse.* Paper presented at the British Sociological conference, Edinburgh.

———. 2000. Confronting sexual abuse: Challenges for the future. In C. Itzen, ed., *Home truths about child sexual abuse.* London: Routledge.

O'Carroll, T. 1980. *Paedophillia, the radical case.* London: Peter Owen.

O'Connell-Davidson, J. 2005. *Children in the global sex trade.* Cambridge, UK: Polity.

O'Dell, L. 2003. The 'harm' story in childhood sexual abuse: Contested understandings, disputed knowledges. In P. Reavey and S. Warner, eds., *New feminist stories of child sexual abuse: Sexual scripts and dangerous dialogues.* London: Routledge.

Ong, N. B. 1986. Child abuse: Are abusing women abused women? In C. Webb, ed., *Feminist practise in women's health care.* Chichester, UK: Wiley.

Packman, J., and J. Randall. 1989. Decision making at the gateway to care. In O. Stevenson, ed., *Child abuse: Professional practice and public policy.* Hemel Hempstead, UK: Havester Wheatsheaf.

Pain, R. 2006. Paranoid parenting? Rematerializing risk and fear for children. *Social and Cultural Geography,* 7:2: April.

Parker, R. 1997. The production and purposes of maternal ambivalence. In W. Hollway, and B. Featherstone, eds., *Mothering and ambivalence.* London: Routledge.

Parton, C. 1990. *Taking child abuse seriously: The violence against children study group.* London: Unwin Hyman.

Parton, N. 1985. *The politics of child abuse.* London: Macmillan.

Payne, M. 2000. *Teamwork in multiprofessional care.* Basingstoke, UK: Macmillan.

Petrovich, M., and D. Templar. 1984. Heterosexual molestation of children who later become rapists. *Psychological Reports,* 54, 810.

Piaget, J. 1950. *The psychology of intelligence.* London: Routledge & Kegan Paul.

Plummer, K. 1981. Paedophilia: Constructing a sociological baseline. In M. Cook and K. Howells, eds., *Adult sexual interest in children.* London: Academic Press.

———. 1995. *Telling sexual stories.* London: Routledge.

Portelli, A. 1997. *The battle of Valle Giulia: Oral history and the art of dialogue.* Madison: Univ. of Wisconsin Press.

Pritchard, C. 2004. *The child abusers: Research and controversy.* Berkshire, UK: Open Univ. Press.

Prout, A., and A. James. 1997. A new paradigm for the sociology of childhood? Provenance, promise and problems. In A. James and A. Prout, eds., *Constructing and reconstructing childhood.* London: Routledge Falmer.

Ramsey-Klawsnik, H., April 1990. *Sexual abuse by female perpetrators: impact on children,* Paper presented at the National Symposium on Child Victimisation, Atlanta, GA

Reavey, P., and S. Warner. 2003. *New feminist stories of child sexual abuse: Sexual scripts and dangerous dialogues*. London: Routledge.

Rendel, M. 2000. The UN Convention on the Rights of the Child and British legislation on child abuse and sexuality. In E. Heinze, ed., *Of innocence and autonomy: Children, sex and human rights*. Aldershot, UK: Ashgate.

Renzetti, C. 1999. The challenge to feminism posed by women's use of violence in intimate relationships. In S. Lamb, ed., *New versions of victims: Feminists struggle with the concept*. New York: New York Univ. Press.

———. 2006. Gender and violent crime. In C. Renzetti, L. Goodstein, and S. Miller, eds., *Rethinking gender, crime and justice: Feminist readings*. CA: Roxbury.

Rezmovic, E., D. Sloane, D. Alexander, and B. Seltser. 1996. *Cycle of sexual abuse: Research inconclusive about whether child victims become adult abusers*. GAO/GGD-96–178. Report to the chairman, subcommittee on crime, committee on the judiciary, House of Representatives, United States.

Rich, A., 1976. *Of woman born*, London UK, Virago

———. 1978. Motherhood: the contemporary emergency and the quantum leap, in A. Rich, 1980, *On lies secrets and silence*, London UK, Virago

Roberts, M. 2001. Childcare Policy. In P. Foley, J. Roche, and S. Tucker, eds., *Children in society: Contemporary theory, policy and practice*. Hampshire, UK: Open Univ. Press.

Roiphe, K. 1994. *The morning after: Sex fear and feminism*. London: Hamish Hamilton.

Rosencrans, B. 1997. *The last secret: Daughters sexually abused by mothers*. Brandon, VT: Safer Society Press.

Rowan, E., J. Rowan, and P. Langelier. 1990. Women who molest children. *Bull. Am. Acad. Psychiatry Law*, 18:1:79–83.

Rush, F. 1980. *The best kept secret: Sexual abuse of children*. NJ: Prentice Hall.

———. 1990. The many faces of backlash. In D. Leidholdt and Raymond, eds., *The sexual liberals and the attack on feminism*. New York: Pergamon.

Russell, D. 1984. *Sexual exploitation: Rape, child sexual abuse and workplace harassment*. Beverly Hills, CA: Sage Focus.

———. 1986. *The secret trauma*. New York: Basic Books/London: Routledge.

Russell, D., and D. Finkelhor. 1984. Women as perpetrators. In D. Finkelhor, ed., *Child sexual abuse: New theory and research*. New York: The Free Press.

Rutter, M. 1972. *Maternal deprivation reassessed*, Baltimore, USA, Penguin Books

Salter-Ainsworth, M. 1991. Attachments and other affectional bonds across the life cycle. In C. Murray-Parkes, J. Stevenson-Hinde, and P. Marris, eds., *Attachments across the life cycle*. London: Routledge.

Saradjian, J. 1996. *Women who sexually abuse children*. UK: Wiley.

Saraga, E. 2001. Dangerous places: The family as a site of crime. In J. Muncie and E. McLaughlin, eds., *The problem of crime*, 2nd ed., London: Sage.

Scott, S. 2001. *The politics and experience of ritual abuse: Beyond belief*. Buckingham, UK: Open Univ. Press.

Scott, S., S. Jackson, and K. Bartlett-Milburn. 1998. Swings and roundabouts: Risk, anxiety and the everyday worlds of children. *Sociology*, 32(4), 689–705.

Scottish Executive. 2003. *It's everyone's job to make sure 'I'm alright': Literature review*, http://www.scotland.gov.uk/Publications/2003/05/17127/21830.

Scully, D., and J. Marolla. 1984. Convicted rapists' vocabulary of motive: Excuses and justifications. *Social Problems*, 31(5) 530–44.

Search, G. 1988. *The last taboo: Sexual abuse of children*. London: Penguin.

Segal, L. 1995. Feminism and the family. In C. Buck and B. Speed, eds., *Gender, power and relationships*. London: Routledge.

————. 1997. A feminist looks at the family. In J. Muncie ed., *Understanding the family*. London: Sage.

Sgroi, S., and N. Sargent. 1993. Impact and treatment issues for victims of childhood sexual abuse by female perpetrators. In M. Elliott, ed., *The last taboo*. London: Longman.

Showalter, E. 1997. *Hystories: Hysterical epidemics and modern culture*. New York: Picador.

Sichtermann, B. 1983. *Femininity, the politics of the personal*. Oxford, UK: Polity.

Sidebottom, P. 2001. An ecological approach to child abuse: A creative use of scientific models in research and practice. *Child Abuse Review*, 10:2:97–112.

Sieber, J. 1993. The ethics and politics of sensitive research. In R. Lee, ed., *Researching sensitive topics*. Beverly Hills, CA: Sage Focus.

Sieber, JE., and B. Stanley. 1988, Ethical professional dimensions of socially sensitive research, *American Psychologist*, 43:49-55

Sinason, V. 1994. *Treating survivors of satanist abuse*. London: Routledge.

Sinclair, R., and R. Bullock. 2002. *Learning from past experience: A review of serious case reviews*. London: DOH.

Skidmore, P. 1995. Just another moral panic? Media reporting of child sexual abuse. *Sociology Review*, April, 4:4:19–23.

Smart, C. 1989. *Feminism and the power of the law*. London: Routledge.

————. 1995. *Law, crime and sexuality*. London: Sage.

————. 1996. Deconstructing motherhood. In E. Bartolaia Silva, ed., *Good enough mothering*. London: Routledge.

Smart, C., and B. Neale. 1999. *Family fragments*. Cambridge, UK: Polity.

Smith, G. 1995. Hierarchy in families where sexual abuse is an issue, in C. Buck & B. Speed eds., *Gender, power and relationships*, London, UK, Routledge

Stainton-Rogers, W. 2000. Theories of child development. In P. Foley, J. Roche, and S. Tucker, eds., *Children in society*. Basingstoke, UK: Palgrave.

Stanko, E. 1985. *Intimate intrusions: Women's experience of male violence*. London: Virago Press.

Steadman, C. 1986. *Landscape for a good woman*. London: Virago Press.

Stock, W. 1998. Women's sexual coersion of men: A feminist analysis. In P. Anderson and W. Struckman-Johnson, eds., *Sexually aggressive women: Current perspectives and controversies*. New York: Guilford.

Summit, R. 1983. The child sexual abuse accommodation syndrome. *Child Abuse and Neglect*, 7, 177–93.

Summit, R., and J. Kryso. 1981. Sexual abuse of children: A clinical spectrum. In L. Constantine and F. Martinson, eds., *Children and sex: New findings and research*. Boston: Little, Brown.

Sykes, G., and D. Matza. 1957. Techniques of neutralization. In J. Muncie, E. McLaughlin, and M. Langan, eds., *Criminological perspectives (1996)*. Buckingham, UK: Open Univ. Press.

Taylor, A. 1998. Hostages to fortune: The abuse of children in care. In G. Hunt, ed., *Whistleblowing in the social services: Public accountability and professional practice*. London: Arnold.

Taylor, L. 1972. The significance and interpretation of replies to motivational questions: The case of the sex offender. *Sociology*, 6, 23–39.

Thomas, T. 2000. *Sex crime: Sex offending and society*. Cullompton, UK: Willan.

Thorne, B. 1992. Feminism and the family. In B. Thorne and M. Yalom, eds., *Rethinking the family: Some feminist questions*. Boston: Northeastern Univ. Press.

Turner, S. 1995. *An investigation of social workers' attitudes towards the sexual abuse of children by women*. Unpublished master's thesis, University of Middlesex, U.K.

Turner, M., and T. Turner. 1994. *Female adolescent sexual abusers: An exploratory study of mother-daughter dynamics with implications for treatment.* Brandon, VT: Safer Society Press.

Turton, J. 2000. Maternal sexual abuse and its victims. *ChildRight,* 165, 17–18.

Turton, J., and L. Haines. 2007. *An investigation into the nature and impact of complaints made against paediatricians involved in child protection procedures.* London: Royal College of Paediatrics and Child Health.

Unassigned authorship. 18 December 2001. Paynes ask Blunkett for 'Sarah's Law', Special Reports, *Guardian Unlimited* http://www.guardian.co.uk/child/story/0,7369,620625,00.html

Valios, N. 2000. Women abuse too. *Community Care,* 14–20 March, 28–29.

———. 2001. Prisoner of the past. *Community Care,* 19–25, April, 15.

Waldby, C. 1989. Theoretical perspectives on father-daughter incest. In E. Driver and A. Droisen, eds., *Child sexual abuse: Feminist perspectives.* London: Macmillan.

Walklate, S. 1989. *Victimology: The victim and the criminal justice process.* London: Unwin Hyman.

———. 2001. *Gender, crime and criminal justice.* Devon, UK: Willan.

Walters, H. 2007. *An introduction to child protection legislation in the UK,* NSPCC, UK: www.nspcc.org.uk/inform/online.

Warner, S. 2000. *Understanding child sexual abuse: Making the tactics visible.* Gloucester, UK: Handsell Publishing.

———. 2001. Disrupting narratives of blame: Domestic violence, child sexual abuse and the regulation of experience and identity. *Psychology of Women Section Review,* 4:1:3–17.

Waterhouse, Sir R. 2000. *Lost in care: The report of the tribunal of inquiry into the abuse of children in care in the former county council areas of Gwynedd & Clwyd since 1974,* http://www.dh.gov.uk/en/Publicationsandstatistics/Publications/PublicationsPolicyAndGuidance/DH_4003097.

Watermann, J., and B. Meir. 1993. Background literature. In J. Watermann et al., eds., *Behind the playground walls: Sexual abuse in pre-schools.* New York: Guilford.

Webster, P. 1975. Matriarchy: A vision of power. In R. R. Reiter, ed., *Toward an anthropology of woman.* New York: Monthly Review Press.

Weeks, J. 1989. *Sex, politics and society: The regulation of sexuality since 1800,* 2nd ed. London: Longham.

Welldon, E. 1988. *Madonna mother whore.* New York: Guilford.

Wilczynski, A. 1995. Child-killing by parents: Social, legal and gender issues. In R. Emerson Dobash, R. Dobash, and L. Noaks, eds., *Gender and Crime.* Cardiff, UK: Univ. of Wales Press.

Williams, L. 1995. Recovered memories of abuse in women with documented child sexual victimisation histories. *Journal of Traumatic Stress,* 8:4:649–73.

Williams, S. J. 1998. Arlie Russell Hochschild. In R. Stones, ed., *Key sociological thinkers.* London: Macmillan.

Winnicott, D. 1964. *The child, the family and the outside world.* London: Penguin.

Witz, A. 1992. *Professions and patriarchy.* London: Routledge.

Wolfers, O. 1993. The paradox of women who sexually abuse children. In M. Elliott, ed., *The last taboo.* London: Longman.

Worrall, A. 1990. *Offending women: Female lawbreakers and the criminal justice system.* London: Routledge.

———. 2002. Rendering women punishable: The making of a penal crisis. In P. Carlen, ed., *Women and punishment.* Devon, UK: Willan.

Wyatt, G., and M. Higgs. 2000. The medical diagnosis of child sexual abuse in Cleveland in 1987: The paediatrician's dilemma. In C. Itzin, ed., *Home truths about child sexual abuse*. London: Routledge.

Yates, C. 1990. A family affair Pt 1: Sexual offences, sentencing and treatment. *Journal of Child Care Law*, 2, 70–76.

Yllo, K. A. 1993. Through a feminist lens: Gender, power and violence. In R. J. Gelles and D. R. Loseke, eds., *Current controversies on family violence*. CA: Sage.

Young, I. M. 1984. Is male gender identity the cause of male domination? In J. Trebilcot, ed., *Mothering*. NJ: Rowman & Allanheld.

———. 1990. *Throwing like a girl and other essays*. Indianapolis: Indiana Univ. Press.

Young, J. 1999. *The exclusive society*. London: Sage.

Young, V. 1993. Women abusers: A feminist view. In M. Elliott, ed., *The last taboo*. London: Longman.

Yow, V. 1994. *Recording oral history*. CA: Sage.

UK ACTS OF PARLIAMENT

Children Act 1989, London, UK, The Stationery Office Limited or online: http://www.opsi.gov.uk/acts/acts1989/Ukpga_19890041_en_1.htm

Children Act 2004, London, UK, The Stationery Office Limited or online: http://www.opsi.gov.uk/acts/acts2004/20040031.htm

Sexual Offences Act 2003, London, UK, The Stationery Office Limited or online: http://www.opsi.gov.uk/acts/acts2003/20030042.htm

Index

Printed in the United States
137693LV00002B/8/P